T0330116

TRANSNATIONAL MIGRATION AND THE NEW SUBJECTS OF WORK

Transmigrants, Hybrids
and Cosmopolitans

Banu Özkazanç-Pan

BRISTOL
UNIVERSITY
PRESS

First published in Great Britain in 2019 by

Bristol University Press
University of Bristol
1-9 Old Park Hill
Bristol
BS2 8BB
UK
t: +44 (0)117 954 5940
www.bristoluniversitypress.co.uk

North America office:
Bristol University Press
c/o The University of Chicago Press
1427 East 60th Street
Chicago, IL 60637, USA
t: +1 773 702 7700
f: +1 773-702-9756
sales@press.uchicago.edu
www.press.uchicago.edu

British Library Cataloguing in Publication Data
A catalogue record for this book is available from the British Library

Library of Congress Cataloging-in-Publication Data
A catalog record for this book has been requested

ISBN 978-1-5292-0454-4 hardcover
ISBN 978-1-5292-0456-8 ePub
ISBN 978-1-5292-0455-1 ePdf

Cover design by Blu Inc
Front cover image: Barth Bailey on Unsplash
Printed and bound in Great Britain by CPI Group (UK) Ltd, Croydon, CR0 4YY
Bristol University Press uses environmentally responsible print partners

Contents

Preface

This book is the result of many years of transnational living, being and belonging, spanning the majority of my childhood and adult life. The language of transnational migration studies has allowed me to theorize and give voice to those experiences and practices that were often found in my own life and experiences. Yet in my doctoral training at a business school, I found that the majority of concepts, frameworks, and tools available to study 'people like me' and many of my colleagues and friends simply did not account for the complexity of transnational lives. Under the guidance of my advisor, Prof. Marta B. Calás, transnationalism and migration studies became important lenses to examine lives that were often not accounted for in most mainstream cross-cultural management and diversity literatures. Over the course of a decade, these frameworks have provided some insights not only in my personal and professional life but also for the direction of my work and the kinds of research questions I have been able to ask.

True to the transnational experiences and subjectivities highlighted in this book, the writing of the book is no different than the very concepts discussed herein. This book was written over the course of one year in Guilford, CT, Boston, MA, Providence, RI, New York City, Istanbul, Turkey, Tokyo, Japan and Sydney, Australia—each place reflecting a space and place that I inhabited long term or for short durations of time. These travels and the transnational modes that accompanied the mobility allowed me to not only see the ways in which being and belonging were taking shape in different contexts, but to also embody it. During the summer of 2018, a trip to a seaside resort in Turkey yielded a conversation with a young adult who had left his home country of Kazakhstan to live and work in the area. He spoke little Turkish but a lot more English—he was a waiter at the restaurant in the resort and his main concern was that the tourists from mostly Arab-speaking Middle East countries had learned Turkish during their extended stays in Turkey and not as much English. Thus, he was barely able to speak with them but still expected to wait on them. In the course of our conversations, he told us about working in Turkey to earn money over the summer while waiting for a visa to go to Estonia where he would study economics in the hopes of fulfilling his dream of immigrating to Canada. This young man's life in that moment of encounter and his hopes and dreams for the future were undoubtedly some of the best memories I have in writing this book—his personhood perhaps best represented by some of the subjectivities highlighted here and impossible to contain solely in the markers of identity and nation.

In all, this book represents an approach to re-thinking difference in a mobile word by way of transnational migration studies—perhaps in the near future, the scholarly field of management and organization studies will re-invent itself to become relevant in a world that is rarely going to slow down for 'theory' to catch-up. And as the social world continues to go through many different transformations, the ideas and frameworks available to study it from transnational migration studies provide important and relevant insights for the scholarly field.

Banu Özkazanç-Pan
Guilford, CT, USA
November 20, 2018

PART I

Introduction and Overview

1

Introduction

Over the course of history, migration, or the movement of people across various geographic and national borders, has resulted in important societal changes across socio-cultural, technological, economic and political dimensions. These movements have brought about opportunities for new combinations of ideas, practices and processes as people live their personal and professional lives at the intersections of multiple social and cultural worlds. At their most immediate, infusions of newcomers to existing societies have brought about significant changes in how people understand themselves and cultural Others. In essence, the mobility of people, ideas and practices has resulted in the emergence of novel mixings that have challenged and expanded on the existing contours of societies. It is no longer possible to speak about homogenous societies but, rather, it is necessary to acknowledge and understand how societies and nations are the result of centuries of people mixing together.

In contemporary times, these mobilities require reconsideration of how individuals are identified as part of a culture, a group or even a nation. Moreover, can we really understand differences between and among people based on nationality, culture or any other dimension in the context of mobility? Sometimes, the best displays of the complex nature of citizenship are during large-scale global events, such as the Olympics or soccer World Cup. In such instances, the intersections of race, ethnicity/heritage, language and citizenship (and privilege) allow consideration of the diversity of societies and patterns of mobility—such as Italian athletes of Somali descent, Korean-American athletes with dual citizenship competing for South Korea, Australians of Greek-descent waiving Greek and Australian flags, and so forth. These mixings of people and cultures are also evidenced in everyday lives through the production and consumption of cultural products, such as books, movies or music, that circulate globally, creating transnationally shared social imaginaries and experiences despite national borders. As a result of these ongoing encounters between and among different groups of people, societies have become transformed, bringing about opportunities to understand 'difference' differently or new ways of understanding one's self and cultural 'Others' in the context of changing social relationships. While such changes may signal positive and emergent opportunities for dialogue and understanding, such as new and novel opportunities for how we theorize the social world and those whose views and lives differ from ours, there has also been a simultaneous 'dark' side to migration and mobilities.

That is, rather than focusing on the broad notion of migration, most conversations and debates have taken shape in relation to particular kinds of people that are migrating: immigrants, refugees, asylum seekers, migrant workers, and others. These debates have taken place over the course of history as social changes resulting from the mobility of various kinds of people have been framed as threats to existing ways of life, national identity and sovereignty, and in need of governing and control (Chatterjee, 2004). Generally adopting xenophobic tones, opponents of generous or lax immigration policies have focused on presumed economic and social consequences resulting from the flow of 'outsiders' or cultural Others into 'their nations' who will 'take jobs', 'commit crimes', 'tax the healthcare system' or 'threaten values'. At the same time, migration has not taken place voluntarily for millions of people. Throughout history, people have been the subject of forced movements. War, slavery, human trafficking, economic desperation, colonialism, political or religious persecution have resulted in the forcible movement of people, upending families, communities, and societies.

In today's cantankerous global political order, various forms of migration have become one of the most polarizing issues, particularly in Western democracies. In the US, intolerant rhetoric about Mexicans, Muslims, immigrants and asylum seekers has resonated with significant portions of society, creating a sense that such groups are 'outsiders within'. In most immediate terms, we are witnessing the horrendous consequences for such migration for children in the US as the current administration has taken up a 'Zero Tolerance' policy that allows the forcible separation of families at the border with Mexico. The images of children in cages meant for animals has resulted in large-scale condemnation and demonstrations in the US and abroad for the immigration policies of the Trump administration. Meanwhile, Europe struggles with the specter of Brexit and the rise of 'nationalist populism' (Gusterson, 2017) amid the Syrian refugee crisis that has come to dominate discussions on immigration policy.

Most recently, initiatives that aim to 'integrate' immigrants and eliminate parallel societies have drawn both praise and ire, including the most recent attempt in Denmark to teach 'Danish values' to 'ghetto' (immigrant) children. Globally, the rise of authoritarian leaders and regimes has brought about new concerns about freedom of movement for certain populations and people at a time when diplomatic relations between nations seem fraught with tensions. At the same time, there has been a growing number of South-South migrations and ensuing changes in the social, economic, and political make-up of 'hosting' nations. While sometimes the focus of these migrations has been on remittances (Ratha and Shaw, 2007), much more research is necessary to understand rising issues around work conditions, for example the challenges around housing, fair wages, and workers' rights in regards to South East Asian migrant workers in Gulf States (Kamrava and Babar, 2012). Interestingly, such migrations have also produced emergent middle classes such as the rising Indian middle class in Dubai (Vora, 2008). In all, such mobilities call attention to the new possibilities around changing work conditions and opportunities while also raising questions around the constitutions of the nation-state in a global context.

Migration in its various forms is only possible if there are clear boundaries, such as those of nation-states, cultural practices, ancestral land claims and other demarcating dimensions. Yet even claiming that people are crossing boundaries assumes a particular version of history: for example, in the US, any movement of people from Central and South America is considered South-North migration. At the same time, it is only in recent history that the states now considered part of the South in the US, such as Texas, were taken by force from Mexico. The same is true in various other contexts around the world in the aftermath of war and conflict: the remnants of the Ottoman Empire were divided up by European powers with consequences of that process continuing into today's Middle East politics and territory conflicts, Japan's occupation of China and Korea followed by Allied Occupation of Japan, the British, Dutch, French and Germans in Africa and the ensuring issues of land ownership, apartheid and poverty among many other examples throughout history. At its core, the very notion of modern-day nation-states occludes histories of imperialism, war, and other forms of conflict and violence that allowed the creation of such states. Thus, speaking about migration in any form requires acknowledging the historic ways in which boundaries and borders were created and continue to be replicated through epistemic, social and material practices including the ways academic research theorizes and examines issues of 'difference' between/among people, cultures and groups.

These global trends, which are both historic and contemporary, have also raised questions around how societies should function in the context of migration—what are ethical concerns and considerations in relation to society when nations have been created by battles, guided by particular narratives of history and myths of homogeneity? In this sense, many questions remain about how mobility impacts the very institutions of society as well as its impact on social, cultural, economic, and political organizations and people. What difference does mobility make for how we understand the world and how people make sense of who they are and cultural 'Others'? And how does mobility impact the ways in which work gets done and how people live their personal and professional lives under conditions of transnationalism?

To examine these and other concerns, this book brings about insights and key concepts from the field of transnational migration studies to bear upon the field of organization studies. In doing so, it offers new frameworks for the study of people on-the-move and organizations through a mobility ontology that foregrounds movement as the natural order of the social world. It also calls into question the ways existing research paradigms and approaches have potentially replicated the creation of boundaries and borders through implicit assumptions about difference, race/ethnicity and belonging. By shifting the ontological premise on which the field of organization studies rests, this book provides novel ways of theorizing difference, people and work beyond the static epistemologies that guide much of the field. To accomplish this, the next section lays out the existing approaches and challenges of the organization studies field as it related to the study of difference, people and work.

Existing approaches to the study of difference

In general, diversity can be defined as those differences of gender, race, ethnicity, sexual orientation, class, among other dimensions, and their influence on one's identity, values and behaviors, and experiences in organizations and across societies (Page, 2008). In the management and organizations studies (MOS) field, the diversity framework has been the dominant approach to the study of people and difference, often outlining ways in which differences make a difference for a variety of topics, such as identity, organizational practices, and so forth. Specifically, scholars have studied various dimensions of diversity across multiple levels of analysis including individuals, groups and organizations (Williams and O'Reilly, 1998) by examining women and racial/ethnic minorities' organizational experiences (Castilla, 2008; van Laer and Janssens, 2011, 2017). Others have considered group dynamics (Van Knippenberg et al., 2004; Joshi and Roh, 2009), effective practices for creating inclusive organizations

(Nishii, 2013), diversity in relation to person–organization fit (Ng and Burke, 2005), and firm performance (Roberson et al., 2017), among many other topics.

While most diversity research has taken shape within the context of single nations, there has also been acknowledgment of globalization as it relates to differences. Here, globalization can be understood as flows of people, financial resources, social practices, cultural forms and technologies between and among nations (Appadurai, 1996). In this context, diversity and difference focused MOS has moved beyond single nation and organizational contexts to examine international human resource management practices including ways to manage diversity in multinationals (Shen et al., 2009; Stahl et al., 2012). In such work, scholars provide insights on culturally-contextualized ways diversity management is taking shape in different nations (Özbilgin and Tatli, 2008; Özbilgin and Chanlat, 2017), such as Denmark (Boxenbaum, 2006; Risberg and Soderberg, 2008; Lauring, 2009), and regions, such as Africa (Nyambegera, 2002; Jackson, 2004) and Asia (Rowley and Harry, 2011), by way of human resource practices (Brewster et al., 2005). Moreover, work that recognizes the mobility of employees across national borders offers insights about managing them (Brewster et al., 2001), how such individuals navigate different cultural identities (van Laer and Janssens, 2014) and the intersectional construction of being 'foreign' in organizations (Wells et al., 2015). These growing concerns in diversity research intersect with existing scholarship in international management focused on developing a globally competitive workforce (Schuler et al., 2002), building (multi)culturally inclusive workplaces (Holvino, 2014; Mor Barak, 2016) and understanding the role of culture in mentoring relationships (Kumar, 2017).

As such, research in international management also attends to issues of globalization, people and difference, but often by deploying a cultural lens influenced by Hofstede's (1984a) seminal work, *Culture's Consequences*. In this work, culture is defined as 'collective programming' of the mind that could be used to distinguish one group of people from another group. Hofstede (1984b) suggests that these cultural values are reflections of national systems of culture and are a big influence on work values (see Beugelsdijk et al., 2017, for an overview). National culture as an explanatory framework for studying and understanding differences in work values became even more influential as additional scholars expanded on the original set of cultural dimensions to provide new frameworks (Smith et al., 1996; Schwartz, 1999). Others have attempted to provide 'better' measures of culture through new concepts: cultural distance or the extent to which 'cultures are similar or different' (Shenkar, 2001: 519).

In recent years, researchers have continued examining the role of national culture in relation to work values (Hofstede, 2003; Taras et al., 2010; Ralston et al., 2017). Other research has focused on the role of cultural intelligence (Chao et al., 2017) and ways to cultivate a global mindset (Gupta and Govindarajan, 2002; Levy et al., 2007) in order to increase cross-cultural competence (Johnson et al., 2006) and transnational competence by way of individual behavioral dimensions (Koehn and Rosenau, 2002).

Acknowledging the movement of people and organizational practices from one nation to another, researchers examining global careers have examined challenges associated with this growing form of employment (Shaffer et al., 2012; Baruch et al., 2016) and examined the transfer of human resource management practices across multinationals (Björkman and Lervik, 2007; Tung, 2016; Edwards et al., 2016) including those that aim to achieve diversity in organizations spanning geographic boundaries (Syed and Özbilgin, 2009). A large number of works that recognize movement of employees focus on expatriate experiences and adjustments (Johnson et al., 2003; Harrison et al., 2004; Nguyen and Benet-Martínez, 2013; Selmer and Lauring, 2015; McNulty and Brewster, 2017) including those of minority expatriates (Pattie and Parks, 2011). Within this vein, researchers have also examined bi-culturals whereby individuals identify with home and host countries (Bell, 1990; Brannen and Thomas, 2010; Thomas et al., 2010; Tadmor et al., 2012), multiculturalism (Adler, 1983) and multicultural employees to understand cultural identity patterns by way of a cultural schema lens (Nguyen and Benet-Martínez, 2010; Yagi and Kleinberg, 2011; Fitzsimmons, 2013) as well as through political ideologies (Peterson et al., 2017).

Taken together, both diversity and the cross-cultural/international management fields attend to difference in the context of globalization and examine the ways differences influence both individuals and organizations in relation to the values, behaviors, and experiences of individuals, and the management and human resource practices adopted by organizations in different cultural contexts. These subfields of MOS differ in their focus of what constitutes difference whereby the diversity field focuses predominantly on issues of gender, race and psychological dimensions, the cross-cultural management field derives its notion of difference from cultural frameworks. In recent years, there has been some convergence between these subfields in relation to human resources management and best practices around the management of diverse, multicultural, multinational organizations. Despite the recognition of difference as an important influencer of professional experiences and organizational practices, the study of difference in MOS as it relates to people has generally arrived out of the worldviews and theoretical formations of the Global North/West.

Critique of existing approaches

On this point, critique from within the MOS field suggests diversity research must move beyond its US-centric assumptions and inflection points in a global context (Bendl et al., 2015) and attend to experiences and topics under-researched in the literature, including immigrants in the US context (Bell et al., 2010), Muslim minorities in Europe (Mahadevan and Mayer, 2017), and diversity practices extant across the globe (Syed and Özbilgin, 2015). Jonsen et al. (2011) suggest research must attend to different types of diversity, such as class, and contexts beyond the US while Nkomo and Hoobler (2014) suggest that concepts like 'multiculturalism' and 'inclusion' guiding US-based human resource management practices and research have become normalized based on particular historic events.

On this point, Faria (2015) calls for decolonizing diversity and attending to its epistemic pluversality in contrast to US-centric approaches that have (mis)appropriated the very subjects of research in the images of Western/Eurocentric rational individuals. Similarly, Calás et al. (2010) attend simultaneously to the epistemic claims made by scholars in the name of diversity and the historically grounded notions of diversity that emerge in local contexts by uncovering the (problematic) ways in which gender and race research travels under globalized capitalism. Deploying postcolonial theory, Kalonaityte (2010) suggests that diversity management approaches are based on assumptions of European racial superiority and therefore, used to justify control of borders and immigration. By way of postcolonial and anticolonial frameworks, Nkomo (2011) highlights the complexities of navigating between culturally relativistic notions of African leadership versus those arriving out of colonial stereotypes. She provides new anticolonial possibilities for conceptualizing on/about 'cultural Others' that cannot be sufficiently represented through existing categories for studying difference.

In a similar vein, contemporary critique of international management research focuses on its guiding epistemological assumptions (Jack et al., 2008) and subjects/subject formation (Özkazanç-Pan, 2008; Jack et al., 2013) in the context of long standing concerns around the appropriateness of deploying 'American' theories in other cultural contexts (Hofstede, 1980, 1983, 1993) and the continued parochial nature of organizational research under globalization (Boyacigiller and Adler, 1991). As Tung (2008a: 41) suggests, there is a 'fallacious assumption of cultural homogeneity ... and cultural stability' in nations over time and calls for researchers to balance cross-national and intra-national diversity to move cross-cultural research forward. Ferner et al. (2005) suggest that transferring US-based 'workforce diversity' initiatives to other geographies of the multinational take shape in the context of institutional pressures and power/interest conflicts. As such, transfer and mobility of people and practices are not simply the movement of resources from one location to another but take shape in the context of power relations (Peltonen, 2006). Consequently, researchers recognize that inclusion of marginalized groups requires a reflexive approach to human resource management (HRM; Mahadevan and Mayer, 2017), alternative way of organizing and performative activities (Janssens and Zanoni, 2014) and organizational reflection to open up possibilities for agency in the face of dominant assimilation discourses targeting cultural Others (Ghorashi and Ponzoni, 2014). Yet to move diversity beyond these critiques and redirect the study of difference and people, it is necessary to attend to the broader, ongoing societal changes taking shape by way of international migration as a condition of human experience across societies (De Haas, 2005; Gold and Nawyn, 2013). In other words, it is time to conceptualize mobility as an ontology rather than a descriptive term.

Transnationalism: the new mobility lens

According to the Migration Policy Institute (MPI, 2017), between 1960 and 2015, international migration/immigration increased more than threefold across the globe, going from 77 million to 244 million people. Immigrants account for about 28% of the population in Australia, 17% in Sweden, 15% of the population in the US and Germany, 13% in the UK, and 12% in France to name a few countries (MPI, 2017). Within this vein, few organization scholars have adopted theoretical frameworks that can attend to the mobile, complex subject and the novel ways in which individuals define and differentiate themselves in the contemporary context of migration and globalization. McKenna et al. (2015) underscore the emergence of the transnational capitalist class and professional elites as relevant for understanding processes of capitalist expansion and globalization. In related work, Skovgaard-Smith and Poulfelt (2017) focus on how transnational professional elites form a sense of identity by drawing upon cosmopolitan experiences and encounters to form a sense of 'non-nationality'. Guided by the mobility turn in social sciences, Özkazanç-Pan and Calás (2015) suggest cultural encounters result in mobile subjectivities that cannot be represented by the extant identity categories of diversity research and offer a 'post-identitarian' approach to underscore the mobile and precarious nature of subjects. Using mobile subjectivities as their lens, Calás et al. (2013) examine business practices across national borders to demonstrate that identity-based intersectional approaches cannot represent or reflect experiences associated with a new ontological state. To this end, Calás and Smircich (2011: 413) note that 'this is a world of mobility and mobilization, of interconnections and networks, but with a "from" and a "to" and a "back again"'.

Taken together, these emergent works provide insights about the mobility of theories on/about diversity and novel ways to conceptualize subjects in an interconnected world. Yet they do not deploy transnational migration as a conceptual framework for redirecting diversity research or attend sufficiently to its guiding assumptions around the constitution of nation, belonging, and difference in society: who emerges as belonging in narratives of nationhood (Bhabha, 1990) and who becomes marginalized. On this note, Özkazanç-Pan (2019) focuses on 'superdiversity', a concept derived from transnational migration studies to suggest that belonging, rather than inclusion, offers insights about the ways in which society and organizations need to change. Narratives on/about nationhood and belonging, and attendant material and social practices reflect not only ongoing changes and tensions in society but also have implications for how we theorize diversity, difference and belonging in the context of organizations—how are categories deployed to study people and difference, and who or what do such ways of 'seeing' limit in terms of understanding the complexity of intersecting lives, work and organizational experiences?

In many ways, transnational migration reflects a new ontology in the world, that of mobility, and thus its assumptions represent a challenge to the static epistemology and comparative methodologies guiding much of contemporary diversity and cross-cultural management research. To address these concerns and offer new directions for MOS research, I derive three key insights from transnational migration studies—*multiscalar global perspective, moving beyond methodological nationalism*, and *historical global conjunctures*—as relevant frames for rethinking difference. These insights reflect opportunities for studying people and difference in novel ways including agentic, reflexive mobile subjectivities as the new subjects of diversity research that emerge in a 'post-identitarian' world.

Specifically, I outline transmigrant, hybrid, and cosmopolitan subjectivities as the new subjects of diversity research. Beyond new subjectivities, mobility ontology requires rethinking the epistemology of multiculturalism, examining inequalities, and redirecting the methodologies adopted to attend to difference. Conceptualizing multiculturalism as the outcome of historic migrations that contributed to nation-building through racialized, ethnicized political subjects provides new opportunities for research that attends to culture and differences broadly. Moreover, the mobility turn also requires understanding the conditions from which and to which subjects move and live their personal and professional lives. These conditions include addressing inequalities in the context of organizations and across social fields. Finally, I expand on mobile methodologies as those approaches that can attend to the movement of people, practices, and ideas in the context of mobility and work. In all, by attending to a different ontology, a mobility ontology, this book offers new possibilities for understanding and studying people on-the-move as the new subjects of work in the context of transnationalism. These new concepts provide insights for scholars interested in understanding how contemporary and historic trends related to transnationalism expand on existing theories and concepts used to study people, organizations, and work.

To accomplish this, the book is organized into three parts and eight chapters.

Part I: Introduction (this chapter) and Overview

Chapter 2: Transnational Migration Studies

This chapter outlines the three main concepts that are derived from transnational migration studies. Transnational migration signifies mobility that not only spans geographies but also space and social fields, allowing scholars to account for and understand how (new) forms of identity, belonging, and nationhood materialize (Baubock and Faist, 2010). In turn, the ongoing societal changes taking shape by way of transnational migration reflect a new reality and social condition, that of mobility and encounters between/among people across relations of difference that are themselves constantly shifting. To expand on new directions for management scholarship that are possible based on transnational migration studies, this chapter identifies three key concepts: *multiscalar global perspective, moving beyond methodological nationalism,* and *global historical conjunctures*. Each of these concepts are expanded on in terms of their main points and contributions to thinking about the new social condition of mobility as it relates to theorizing people, difference and work—an endeavor that is the focus of the following three chapters.

Part II: New Subjects: Transmigrants, Hybrids and Cosmopolitans

The three chapters in this section focus on new concepts of understanding identities and self that are derived from the three key concepts of transnational migration studies as outlined in Part I.

Chapter 3: Transmigrants

This chapter focuses on transmigrants, a particular kind of transnational personhood derived from the ideas that identity is not fixed, and people can act in reflexive, agentic ways to craft their sense of self based on context (Özkazanç-Pan and Calás, 2015). It then compares this approach to personhood with existing notions of identity and self in the MOS and cross-cultural management research fields. Specifically, diversity literature that acknowledges and examines dynamic aspects of identities does so by focusing on identity formation and using intersectional lenses (Özbilgin et al., 2011; Tatli and Özbilgin, 2012; Atewologun et al., 2015). Similarly, attempts to capture the multi-faceted and dynamic nature of people in the cross-cultural management field are dominated by concerns over whether individuals are blending national culture and economic ideology in ways that converge or diverge in organizations as a means to understand how individuals may be crafting their own set of values beyond culture (see Witt, 2008). Based on these trends, the chapter provides comparative critique on existing approaches in the MOS and cross-cultural management field that aim to speak of a diverse and globally-mobile subject. The focus here is the foundational assumptions of this existing work as derived from static views of the world and the potential for new notions of self available from transnational migration studies: transmigrants as agentic, subjectivities who craft their notions of self through their ways of being and ways of belonging in the social world. The chapter concludes with the implications of such a mobile understanding of self for work and organizational life.

Chapter 4: Hybrid Selves

This chapter focuses on hybrid selves, as another kind of transnational self that exists in the social world due to transnational migration. This concept that also has currency in postcolonial traditions (see Özkazanç-Pan, 2008) in addressing how people may craft notions of self that combine existing elements of their cultures, experiences, and identities into new ways of being in the world. Hybrid signifies a new kind of self that arises as a result of the distinct context, experiences, and set of social and material practices that a person engages in to understand themselves and those around them. While there are many ways to define hybrid, here I deploy it as those novel socio-cultural transformations, combinations, and 'mixings' that take shape at the moment of cultural encounter. Hybrid selves form differently even if facing the same set of circumstances and conditions—studying the everyday lives of business people can elucidate the repertoires of actions that they embody and eschew. By outlining the main tenets of hybrid selves, this chapter challenges conceptualizations of 'self' that are based on static notions of identity which limit how we can understand people. It provides examples and comparative illustrations of hybrid selves and contrasts them with research that aims to study similar people in MOS and cross-cultural management. In doing so, the chapter points out main differences between hybrid selves and bi-cultural or multicultural notions of identity that generally offer hyphenation as a solution to the complex ways people may understand themselves, such as African-American and British Muslim.

Chapter 5: Cosmopolitans

This chapter introduces the third novel concept derived from transnational migration studies for understanding people under conditions of mobility, namely cosmopolitans, and offers two critical insights. The first contribution challenges the notion of cosmopolitanism within the cross-cultural management field as referencing people who have a global mindset and are 'citizens of everywhere and nowhere' (Story and Barbuto Jr., 2011). In contrast to this idea of cosmopolitanism, a transnational migration studies offers a multiscalar perspective that uncovers the granularity and performative aspects of this concept inclusive of its ethical dimensions. The second contribution focuses on the ways in which 'global nomad' as a particular example of cosmopolitanism challenges financialized notions of diversity in the context of organizations and neo-liberalism. In other words, it challenges the idea that diversity is only 'good' for organizations if it contributes positively to performance. This approach is generally known as the business case for diversity. Rather, global nomad speaks to issues of agency and choice in how people craft their lives and work arrangements in the context of and in opposition to capitalism. By addressing these elements, this chapters opens up possibilities for (re)thinking the ways people construct their sense of self and their work with an emphasis on the ethical dimensions of such acts.

Part III: Transnational Approaches: New Directions and Challenges for the Field

Building on the prior three chapters and their engagement with new subjects, the next three chapters provide critique and new directions for broader issues in MOS and cross-cultural management that need attention including multiculturalism, inequality and mobile methodologies.

Chapter 6: Diversity Research After Mobility: Multiculturalism

This chapter focuses explicitly on the concept of multiculturalism by providing critique and offering new ways to proceed in research. It does so by first examining existing approaches to multiculturalism within the MOS and cross-cultural management field. Specifically, the critique focuses on the fact that when research addresses multiculturalism, it does so as an add-on to an existing self such that the multicultural self is understood as the result of identifying with more two sets of cultural and, to an extent, political values. Despite their aims to offer insights into the complexity of multicultural people and their experiences, such approaches neither attend to power dimensions of race and ethnicity as they relate to multiculturalism nor to the structural inequalities that people with and without migrant histories face in their lives and work settings among other organizations. To move forward, the chapter discusses how multiculturalism in the context of diversity research must attend to historic formations and their present-day manifestations in relation to the possibilities of subjectivity: what kinds of selves are possible for whom and under what conditions in organizations? By way of this question and building on the key insights of transnational migration studies in relation to new subjects of research, this chapter puts forth new ways of thinking or theorizing about multiculturalism and engaging in research to examine it in the context of work and organizations.

Chapter 7: Inequalities on the Move

As the second focal point in providing new directions for MOS and cross-cultural management scholarship, this chapter focuses explicitly on inequalities to outline why and how they need much more attention in organizational research. The starting point of this chapter is examination of why 'diversity work' or practices to become more inclusive in organizations continues to be necessary in the context of multicultural societies. It then moves onto discuss power relations as relevant to the replication and emergence of inequalities in organizations, something that is not examined sufficiently in current scholarship on diversity and cross-cultural management. The chapter then moves on to outline how future diversity scholarship requires an ethical commitment to tracing the formation of multiscalar inequalities within organizational practices and policies that may be producing and/or replicating them. The chapter concludes by suggesting that the mobility turn in social sciences is not a celebratory one to suggest that everyone moves but, rather, a serious engagement with the interrelated relations of power, inequality and dispossession taking shape in a multiscalar fashion as people move either out of choice, force or need in relation to work and organizations. In all, the chapter focuses on the relevance of inequality for scholarship on people and difference that span social fields in work contexts across geographies.

Chapter 8: Mobile Methodologies

This third and final chapter on new directions for MOS and cross-cultural management focuses explicitly on methodologies. It starts off by noting that transnational approaches contribute a multiscalar understanding and analysis of mobile subjectivities that attending requires moving beyond comparative lenses. These new trends require 'reclassifying existing data, evidence, and historical and ethnographic accounts that are based on bounded or bordered units so that transnational forms and processes are revealed' (Khagram and Levitt, 2007: 2). To clarify, a transnational paradigm does not discount the importance of the nation-state but, rather, holds it as a precarious achievement and construction made possible by discourses of difference and belonging. Yet the nation-state and, thus, 'cultural values' as reflections of nation-states cannot be the starting point for an analysis that aims to understand subjectivities which move across scales and the specificity of experiences associated with mobile encounters. This chapter provides examples of work that can attend to these issues under the notion of 'mobile methodologies'. Under this approach, researchers move with the research object/subject over time, place, and space as needed to understand the assembling of transnational lives, experiences, and practices. The chapter contrasts these approaches with existing works within diversity and cross-cultural management research that adopt comparative and static methods that are unable to attend to mobile subjects. In sum, the chapter offers critique and new directions for methodologies that can be used to study transnational subjects.

Chapter 9: Imagining a Transnational Future for Research on Differences

This chapter examines offers new directions for organizational scholarship based on the key concepts derived from transnational migration studies and applied to notions of self, culture, and work. Fundamentally, transnational modes of thinking and analyzing require us to consider the composition and coming together of society rather than a reflection of the boundaries/boundedness of nation-states. They provide insights as to what citizenship means beyond an accident of birth and turn our gaze to the ways in which historical conjunctures impact contemporary economic arrangements, political debates, and cultural institutions. For organization scholars who want to study diversity and cross-cultural management and attend to difference, transnational modes provide insights as to new ways of understanding people in the form of mobile subjectivities and move us to consider the question of who/what the subject of management research is. By relying on new ontologies and epistemologies available from a transnational migration studies framework, the chapter offers insights about how the social world is being made and remade, and the consequences of such action and intention for the (organizational) lives of people around the world. In doing so, it opens up vistas for new research questions, agendas, and approaches to guide organizational scholars and scholarship.

Transnational Migration Studies

In this chapter, I outline three key concepts derived from transnational migration studies and use them in the following chapters to expand on existing notions of subjectivity and personhood derived from static ontologies. As a starting point, transnational migration studies derives from migration studies, which is a field of inquiry examining the multiple ways individuals move between/among places and nations to engage in various kinds of social, cultural, economic, and political activities (Levitt et al., 2003; Levitt and Glick Schiller, 2004; Vertovec, 2009; Kretsedemas et al., 2013; Waldinger, 2013). Following seminal contributions by Portes (1997) and Portes et al. (1999) that examined transnational dimensions of migration research and concurrent with the mobility turn in social sciences, a transnational approach to migration studies has now become an important analytic lens for the study of mobility, people, and social inequalities (Faist, 2013).

By considering the contours of society and the social, cultural, economic, and political activities taking place across borders (Waldinger and Fitzgerald, 2004), a transnational lens allows examination of the mechanisms through which nations are defined and particular people, histories, and cultures become normalized as part of the nation while 'Others', inclusive of their histories and cultures, become marginalized or erased. Moreover, it allows reconsideration of existing categories of analysis related to people, specifically in relation to race and ethnicity. Transnational migration studies challenges static notions of identity and derived categories of subjectivity based on race and ethnicity as these concepts reflect fundamentally reified social groupings and racialized power relations (see for example DuBois, 1903, 1940; also Bonilla-Silva, 2006; Gilroy, 1993; Hall, 1994). Consequently, this approach challenges existing categories that have been used to study and define people and communities and, by extension, society (this topic is further expanded on in Chapter 6). Transnationalism provokes consideration of how societies take shape over time and continue to function given that notions of societal replication are problematic—no longer are the members of society homogenous and static; rather, they are constantly in a state of becoming and relationality.

In this sense, the notion of transnational is not (only) a signifier but an ontological reality that reflects or speaks to the mobility condition defining the lives and experiences of many people. Perhaps it is best to juxtapose 'transnational' with 'national' in the study of migration given that much of the literature until the work of Portes and others focused on the movement of people from one nation to another—a movement between and across nations. That is not to say that currently there is no work being done adopting a nation-based approach to the study of migration but, rather, that the focus has expanded beyond the physical location and movement of people to social spheres which exist in fields. As such, *transnational* migration focuses on mobility that not only spans geographies but also space and social fields. This focus allows scholars to account for and understand how (new) forms of identity, belonging, and nationhood materialize. In turn, the ongoing societal changes taking shape by way of transnational migration reflect a new ontological condition, that of mobility and ongoing encounters between/among people across relations of difference that are themselves constantly shifting.

These ongoing exchanges provide new opportunities for understanding difference and, as such, can yield insights for redirecting diversity theorizing and research in MOS and international management but also more broadly in the social sciences. Rather, it is a question and concern about how to theorize and pay attention to the ways in which people craft their lives in a world that is constantly moving and shifting. To expand on new directions for scholarship attending to the intersections of difference, culture and work, I focus on three key conversations taking shape within transnational migration studies: *multiscalar global perspective, methodological nationalism* and *global historical conjunctures*. While these are in no way exhaustive conversations, they provide a framework for rethinking the assumptions of extant theories that aim to speak about/for culture, difference, and work.

Multiscalar global perspective

In this section, I focus on several different concepts that simultaneously contribute to the multiscalar global perspective. The first of these is transnational social fields, the second being a focused analysis of power and inequality, and the third being superdiversity. I expand on each of these areas to demonstrate how collectively and simultaneously they provide an analytic lens to understand the emergent of transnationalism as a way of life, whether out of choice or force.

Over the years, several debates and discussions have taken shape within the field of migration studies. Perhaps the most relevant for re-theorizing diversity and cross-cultural research is the discussion around social fields and scale. Social fields can be defined as 'sets of multiple interlocking networks of social relationships through which ideas, practices and resources are unequally exchanged, organized and transformed' (Levitt and Glick Schiller, 2004: 9; also Basch et al., 1994). The idea of the social is quite relevant in how individuals and communities not only relate and link to each other, but how tastes, ideas and ideologies, practices, and other embodied forms traverse the globe. Social fields as a concept also lays the foundation for research into transnational social movements as people and communities share common beliefs, ideologies, and praxis to engage in social and political change (Smith et al., 1997).

Transnational social fields take shape when actors are connected to each other through direct and indirect relations across social fields while *national social fields* are the result of actors and their relations and relationship-making taking place within national boundaries (see Glick Schiller et al., 1992). As a conceptual lens, transnational social fields allow examination of the ways in which migrants are embedded in multi-layered and sited social fields inclusive of people who move as well as those that stay behind (Levitt and Jaworsky, 2007; Levitt and Glick Schiller, 2004). By focusing on the back and forth aspects of migration and moving away from simplistic national comparisons, transnational migration studies' scholars aim to understand nuanced differences between people's ways of being and ways of belonging. To clarify, *ways of being* refers to the actual social relations and practices that individuals engage in, while *ways of belonging* references the practices that 'signal or enact an identity which demonstrates a conscious connection to a particular group' (Levitt and Glick Schiller, 2004: 11). Importantly, this analytic approach differentiates between existence of transnational social networks and consciousness of being embedded in them: the act of relating and awareness of the implications of the act reflect a transnational sense of self.

The subject of analysis in this mode is the transnational self or transmigrant (Glick Schiller, 1999; Guarnizo, 1997), who comes into existence within a social field spanning multiple and interrelated scales including the local, national, regional, and the global in contrast to existing only in bounded nation-states. On this point, Glick Schiller (Levitt and Glick Schiller, 2004: 1008) states, 'without a concept of the social, the relations of power and privilege exercised by social actors based within structures and organizations cannot be studied or analyzed'. Consequently, the starting point for understanding transmigrants as emergent selves is simultaneously power relations and social fields. The interdependent nature of power relations and social fields exemplifies a multiscalar analysis of subjects whereby people with and without migrant histories are conceptualized as existing within mutually constituting personal and institutional networks across relations of power (Caglar and Glick Schiller, 2015; Glick Schiller, 2015). By allowing consideration of both mobility and stasis, this perspective considers the relationship between those who arrive and those who are considered 'locals'. The arrival of individuals and groups necessitates changes and reconsiderations on the part of the host society in various realms including the cultural, economic, and geopolitical (Capetillo-Ponce and Kretsedemas, 2013).

In the contemporary context, transnational analysis of social fields can provide insights as to those habits of the mind and practice that not only take shape in one location but also how they become something else on arriving in another context. Moreover, the idea of power and unequal are also defining features of this mode of analysis. This *notion of inequality* becomes fundamentally important in that the exchanges which define social fields do not and cannot take shape in power and political vacuums—rather as Goldring (1998) points out through the notion of 'transnationalism from below', by its very nature transnationalism is a conversation about the shaping of politics and society. Consequently, the distribution of social, political, and cultural capital as a condition of transnationalism needs attending as well as the ways in which migration and immigration become discourses with particular positive or negative valences.

Moreover, a multiscalar approach focuses on how global economic arrangements impact all people albeit in differentiated ways such that displacement and dispossession of land and labor are conditions of globalized capitalism (Glick Schiller, 2015). Yet, by analytically segregating groups by ethnicity or other dimensions of difference, a hallmark of much MOS research, we risk adopting a myopic approach that cannot fully account for shared experiences and interrelated social dynamics. Given that locales and cities are made up of people who are differentially embedded in economic restructuring and development efforts, understanding their *ways of being and belonging* across social fields and scales is vital to new theorizing about society and ongoing social relationships. In effect, the multiscalar lens derives analytic rigor from focusing not only on the formation of self and communities across social fields but also attends to the very nature and meaning of those engagements while acknowledging the role of power, structures and emergent inequalities.

As a final and third element, the transnational migration perspective reformulates the very foundation of society. It allows consideration for how the intersections of mobility, stasis, and social fields across scales produce a new societal condition, that of '*superdiversity*', which can be defined as 'a condition ... distinguished by a dynamic interplay of variables among an increased number of new, small and scattered, multiple-origin, transnationally connected, socio-economically differentiated and legally stratified immigrants' in different nations and societies (Vertovec, 2007: 1024). Superdiversity as the new defining condition of societies derived from transnationalism provides analytic rigor for understanding the ways in which individuals are simultaneously anchored in new lands and pivoting back and forth between these lands and others (Levitt and Glick Schiller, 2004; Waldinger, 2013). The anchoring and pivoting take shape through transnational kin networks and communications that are maintained through different stages of migration (Park and Waldinger, 2016). Moreover, such anchoring and pivoting are also made possible by new technologies and platforms including emergent opportunities to engage in paid labor—new possibilities emerging for people who are deemed illegal or unable to find 'legal' work to engage in economic activities across social fields. Because of these social, economic, political, and cultural activities, each state around the world represents coming together within place and time of the multiple intersecting array of networks that can be analyzed as transnational social fields (Glick Schiller, 2015: 2276, 2278). Yet to attend to these forms of existence and society requires an approach that is sensitive to the multi-sited and situated nature of people and their lives.

Moving beyond methodological nationalism

If mobility is the new ontological condition of society, then the multiscalar analytic lens can be considered a new epistemic approach to theorize it. But missing still is the methodology or a theory of methods derived from theories about the mobility condition. Put differently, while it is important to recognize that the very concepts of self and society now exist under conditions of transnational mobility, attending to their various dimensions also requires a methodological shift (see Amelina et al., 2012 for overview of available methodologies; Glick Schiller, 2010). Given that the new theories of a world on-the-move reformulate the concept of society as no longer equated with or confined by boundaries of a single nation, what methodological considerations are necessary to 'study' the phenomenon? How can we move beyond a 'container theory of society' (Levitt and Glick Schiller, 2004: 8) and reconsider both the nature and location of society? Despite the relevance and importance of these concerns, one of the main challenges facing migration studies is that scholars still rely on specific national contexts as their unit of analysis and, more problematically, use these examples to generalize other migrant experiences.

These approaches derive from *methodological nationalism* or the assumption that the nation-state reflects the natural order and political form of society (Wimmer and Glick Schiller, 2002). Consequently, the starting unit of analysis is the nation followed closely by the person moving: the migrant. There is an assumed linearity and transitive property—migrants can be identified as belonging to a particular home country but living or working in a host country. The home country is identified with a particular kind of migrant while the host country is identified with 'locals' or natives. The discourse of this approach is generally about who is moving and where they are moving—the back and forth experiences are not considered given that the starting point of the analysis is the leaving of a home country and the arrival into a host country. The notions of home and host go unchallenged with little examination of the existence of historically, politically, and culturally derived differences in migrant experiences. Rather, there is a desire to compare migrant experiences across different societies while leaving intact that very notion of society which migration challenges.

For Glick Schiller (2010: 3), this approach does not allow scholars to 'link their descriptions of migrant local and trans-border connections to analyses of new flexible modes of capital accumulation and the contemporary neo-liberal restructuring of space, self and modes of social legitimation'. In other words, the ways in which migrant experiences are identified and compared across different contexts does not consider the ways in which such experiences take shape in the landscape of neoliberalism and its attendant economic, political, and social structures. At the same time, scholars still assume that 'boundedness, rootedness and membership in a single national, ethnic or religious group are the natural order of things' (Levitt, 2012: 493). Such default categories and conceptual tools prevent a full understanding of the changing nature of societies and the reimagining of the cultural institutions of nation-states that is taking shape. Methodological nationalism normalizes stasis and does not attend to 'social fields of differential power' (Glick Schiller and Salazar, 2013) whereby regulatory and governance mechanisms of nation-states allow particular travelers to move freely (such as a highly educated tech worker or particular kinds of tourists) while stigmatizing and even criminalizing others (a low wage worker; 'illegal immigrants').

It is necessary to move *beyond a comparative approach* in order to understand experiences and formations of self and examine how such experiences and formations change the contours of nation-states. The epistemological shift away from nation-based concepts of self coupled with appropriate methodologies that can 'follow' their subject/object of study allow examination of superdiversity both as a concept and context (Meissner, 2015), voice meaning and assumptions underlying national border crossings for those involved (Kalir, 2013), understand composition of ties among second and third generation immigrants (Crul, 2016), and consider dimensions other than ethnicity, such as religion, that guide incorporation into societies (Glick Schiller et al., 2006). In effect, the multiscalar global lens requires considerable focus on the uneven nature of development, economic, and social policies that result in unequal division of resources and cultural changes across various scales—all issues that cannot be studied with existing methods derived from static ontologies and reified epistemologies. To attend to the complexity, specificity, and fluidity of these issues requires methodologies that are also mobile with their object/subject of studies. These include narrative or biographical approaches that trace self-formations and community development across social fields, textual analyses that follow ideas or practices, storytelling with multiple viewpoints, or visual analyses of traditions (such as veiling practices, hairstyles, habits of dress) among others to understand how such objects/subjects move and what happens when they arrive in different places. While these are methods, they are derived from the epistemic aims and conceptual frameworks of transnational, multiscalar research. By moving beyond methodological nationalism, scholars can debunk notions that societies and nation-states are homogenous until migrants enter/ disrupt them as such assumptions obscure the nation-building discourses, policies, and practices that defined post-war nations (Wimmer and Glick Schiller, 2002)—a political act that imbues the researcher with a particular positionality in the process of studying mobility and people.

Yet there is more reason to move beyond methodological nationalism. While ineffective in studying transnational modes of being and belonging, this approach is also fundamentally problematic in its assumptions about race and multiculturalism. Not only is the nation-based approach theoretically bounded and limited in what it can 'theorize' or see, its foundation is a society that is static until someone or some community enters 'it'. In other words, the society that underlies methodological nationalism is fundamentally an imagined one (Anderson, 1983)—it is an assumed homogenous space, narrated by the dominant groups or as Bhabha suggests in his juxtaposition, 'the language of those who write of it and the lives of those who live it' (1990: 1). In other words, the methodological approach based on nation as the analytic unit is more than a method or tool for the researcher—it is also a political practice that foregrounds a particular version of nationhood and nationality. This is also evident in scholars who want to set limits on or bound transnational social fields so as to be able to study them but, in doing so, they replicate a focus on the migrant—as if such a person exists without pre-conceived notions of nationhood and static borders (for example, see Boccagni, 2012).

As a point of contrast, mobile methods challenge nation-building efforts and origin stories whose basic premise is common ancestry and history among its people. Such methods also provide insights for challenging rising neo-nationalist discourses in democratically elected authoritarian regimes (Kendall-Taylor et al., 2017) that gain authority and credibility by referencing an imagined past of cultural unity, national sovereignty, and shared faith. As researchers, understanding the challenge that methodological nationalism poses for scholarly work requires reflecting on assumptions related to race, history, and modernity. On this point, Chernilo suggests that the 'substantive problem that a "social theory of the nation-state" must tackle is understanding the position and legacy of the nation-state in modernity' (2006: 6).

Consequently, the role of the researcher in examining transnational communities and social fields, structures of inequality, and superdiversity becomes quite relevant. In this vein, the next section focuses on global historical conjunctures as the third relevant conversation taking shape in transnational migration studies.

Global historical conjunctures

In their seminal publication, Held et al. (2000) focus on contemporary social, cultural, technological, economic, and political transformations, and underscore that various theories have been posited to explain and analyze these changes under the notion of globalization. In the realm of migration studies, these global transformations have resulted in discussion around their social and economic consequences for migrants and nation-states (Castles et al., 2013). Specifically, such changes have impacted both the intensity and location of global production networks, brought about changes in governance mechanisms across scales, and provided opportunities for social movement while also constraining the mobility of particular groups of people. More urgently, the changing modes and nature of manufacturing and service industries globally coupled with the economic (re)structuring demands of global capitalism have produced widely varying opportunities for social mobility (Harvey, 2003, 2006).

In this sense, *global historical conjunctures* reflects a conversation about the possibilities for dignity and work in a world that has been fractured and remade by colonial and imperial powers and, most recently, under the auspices of neoliberalism. Therefore, no theories about or methods to study the mobile world inclusive of new formations of self can take shape without contextualizing and examining the historic transformations across socio-cultural, technological, economic, and political dimensions— and how these transformations have impacted the structuring of societies and economies. The experiences of people and communities in this regard cannot be decoupled from shared and divergent histories of oppression, dispossession, capital accumulation, and work intensification as experienced across transnational social scales.

As a concept, global historical conjunctures is an 'approach to history that places transformations in political and social transformations within an analysis of dominant forms of the accumulation and concentration of wealth and power' (Glick Schiller, 2015: 2278). To understand how individuals enact, react, and ascribe agency to their actions in the context of global transformation is a relevant part of transnational migration studies. As such, by tracing the social, cultural, political, and economic trajectories that emerge for different people as transformations take shape can yield insights as to the possibilities for change and social justice (Banerjee-Guha, 2010). This is both an epistemic and methodological concern and, thus, is presented here as the third point arriving out of transnational migration studies. In other words, global historical conjunctures provides both the historical lens and context for any analysis of a transnational nature.

One of the most important issues to emerge in this context has been the intensification of dispossession (Harvey, 2003) or the capital accumulation process across scales through which property, resources, and land are seized from those who possessed them (Glick Schiller, 2015). Such dispossessions have taken on a transnational mode and are emblematic of the structural changes impacting cities (Sassen, 2011) and people (Hall, 2013; Prudham, 2007). Historically and in contemporary times, the loss of land experienced by indigenous and other 'native' groups at the hands of corporations and governments has been particularly relevant. The denial of history and epistemic authority in relation to such groups has allowed for the simultaneous erasure of their claims and the emergence of nation-states through 'purified' accounts of culture, citizenship, and history (Latour, 2012). These actions have resulted in the creation and replication of significant social and economic inequalities across different scales in a transnational sphere. In contemporary terms, it also allows consideration for the ways in which multinational corporations can alter the conditions and possibilities for mobility through their organizational practices and political activities (Levy, 2008; Özkazanç-Pan, 2018).

Only by understanding the different histories associated with people and lands can we begin to address the conditions under which change and agency become possible. To this end, the notion of global historical conjunctures allows consideration for the ways in which new and former relations of power impact the choices, conditions, and experiences available to people. It is a conversation about the intersections of possibilities for belonging to a particular place despite being denied legal recognition, economic power, or social status. Moreover, this approach places history and global transformations as central to contemporary analyses of society and contributes further to dismantling the 'people without history' myth perpetuated by colonial powers and imperial nations (Wolf, 2010). Consequently, we are all *with history* but particular stories about self and the past have become dominant while silencing or marginalizing others.

In the context of mobility, encounters between and among people can result in new histories emerging while at the same time allow examination for the ways in which there may be shared experiences of dispossession, economic disparities, and neoliberal development projects. Understanding the role of historic transformations can serve as a foil to ahistoric conceptualizations of nation, citizenship, and belonging that allow for the denial of rights, land claims, and epistemic authority of marginalized people. This is particularly relevant in a time when immigration and transnationalism have become politicized with the most immediate repercussions being felt by refugees who have been described as security threats (Isotalo, 2009). The impending 'migrant crisis' in Europe as well as the plight of South and Central Americans coming into the US via the Mexican border are two high profile examples, resulting from war, economic insecurity, and everyday violence. Yet these examples are only two of many across time and history, taking shape differently for each community and group of people whose lives have been upended by the nexus of neoliberalism, imperialism, and coloniality in the past and present.

In democracies and authoritarian regimes alike, the proposed threats arising from such people and populations are created through discourses of fear and misinformation, giving legitimacy to efforts at concentrating power in particular state apparatus or individuals. By 'speaking-back' to ahistoric notions of nation and difference, transnational paradigms allow for fruitful and difficult discussions around society, rights, and belonging. They also provide frameworks for rethinking sacred concepts—like nation—that have oft been the foundation of theories about people and differences. With these thoughts in mind, the next section summarizes the main points and contributions of transnational migration studies to theories about people and difference, highlighting their potential for a new way of thinking about the intersections of people, work, and organizations under conditions of mobility.

Summary

In sum, migration studies in a transnational mode provides important insights for developing our thinking on diversity and difference in MOS and international management. To that end, the conversations taking shape in migration studies, including those around a multiscalar global perspective, methodological nationalism and historical global conjunctures, provide new ways of theorizing and doing research focused on people and differences. The main ideas underlying a multiscalar global perspective are threefold. First, there is a concerted effort to change the level of analysis from only local or only global to social fields that span various fields. By changing the analytic focus in this way, the idea is to study and understand how people craft lives that are not delimited by particular (and fictional) boundaries. Transnational social fields speak to those ways of being and ways of belonging that are based on agency—while the conditions under which people may work and live their lives be limited by particular choices, this is certainly not the only defining factor in relation to their experiences. Rather, agency is theorized as those actions and opportunities that allow people to craft a sense of self or multiple self-formations beyond the immediate context in which they live and/ or work. It is a conversation about experiences and self-formations that transcend physical location through technology, community relationships, and history.

Second, there is concerted focus on the forms and mechanisms through which transnationalism intersects with various kinds of inequalities and power relations. This is perhaps one of the most important elements to note in that the formation of different kinds of selves does not take shape in a neutral manner or in a vacuum. Rather, the possibilities for living across transnational social fields is predicated to an extent by various inequalities taking shape globally and begs the question of why and how people move—labor market discrimination, lack of jobs, gender, race or ethnic-based violence, war, persecution, and so forth. These are some of the main reasons people may be forced to move into other places and stay there for indeterminate amounts of time, for example, the Syrian refugees in Lebanon, Turkey, Jordan and other places, or the Rohinga community that has been persecuted and forced to flee their lands, living in horrible conditions in tent cities. With the advent of climate change and super-storms, refugees from Hurricane Katrina are still living in various different states in the US beyond Louisiana with many of them unable to find stable jobs. In all, a large amount of mobility comes about from existing inequalities or leads to further inequalities while a smaller portion may be attributable to choice—moving due to job preferences and opportunities arising from skill sets or experiences. It is important to acknowledge both sets of mobilities in any theory about people and differences.

The third element of a multiscalar global perspective is the new condition of society—namely superdiversity—that provides the opportunity to understand novel and new combinations of people that will arise but also to reconsider the ways in which society has been theorized. Superdiversity as a defining feature of societies not only challenges the extant notion of society as a container of people but it also provides a sense of dynamism. Societies are never static and, consequently, any cultural notions ascribed to a particular society must also be mutable. Yet this is generally where many existing theories of society and nation falter in that the underlying foundation is a homogenous society where there are entrances and exits in the human form of migrants and in the legal form of immigrants. This notion forces us to conceive of society as in flux and made up of not only communities that are physically co-located but also those that are elsewhere—superdiversity as the foundation for society revokes any attempt to define boundaries and borders, and perhaps this is its most powerful contribution. The precarious nature of boundary setting is highlighted as attempts to delimit who is part of which society and in which contexts becomes questioned.

In moving to the second contribution of transnational migration studies, the focus is on the methodological issues associated with adopting the nation as the level and focus of analysis. Rather, the goal is to first debunk the primacy of the nation as the starting point in any conversation about society and culture, and then to understand the ways in which mobile methodologies can provide insights about various phenomena. If we move away from a linear understanding of history and society, then we can no longer equate society and nation as representative of the various communities of people and their experiences. In fact, methodological nationalism becomes fundamentally a flawed approach to understanding the mobility condition and its consequences for people, differences, and culture. By providing alternatives in terms of methods, transnational migration studies offers new avenues for research and study in the context of mobility.

The last contribution arising from transnational migration studies expanded on in this book is the focus on history and historical conjunctures as an important defining factor for understanding how mobility conditions may arise. Over time, the rise and fall of colonial empires and imperial aspirations have crafted a world where the relationships of dependence between Global North/West and Global South were asymmetric—today, such asymmetry continues not only across different nation-states but also within them. The nexus of neoliberalism, nationalism, and climate change have brought about major fractures in societies across the world with some nations literally sinking under water. With growing concerns over totalitarian regimes, clamping down on media, and the weakening of democratic institutions, there is much to be concerned about in relation to the kinds of opportunities that certain people will have in regard to their lives and work. The coming together of these different events in the context of technological advances could potentially also allow for new forms of democratic and participative governance to rise. In fact, the growth of progressive social movements in the US in the age of President Trump demonstrate that historical conjunctures also provide opportunities for new paths to be forged and new mobilities to be possible in relation to how people can and want to live their lives.

In all, these points summarize the various and specific contributions of transnational migration studies to our thinking about people, difference, and culture. In Part II, I expand on these ideas to provide discussion on the new kinds of subjectivities arising from a transnational migration lens and the relevance of these new selves for rethinking people, differences, and culture in management and organization studies. Chapter 3 focuses on transmigrants and outlines the epistemological challenges it poses for existing approaches to the study of people in the diversity and cross-cultural management fields. The chapter provides insights about transmigrants in order to move the field beyond static notions of identity and difference.

PART II

New Subjects: Transmigrants, Hybrids and Cosmopolitans

3

Transmigrants

This chapter focuses further on subjectivities arriving out of the new mobility ontology in a broad sense while the following two chapters outline specific forms that transmigrants can take. If a transnational paradigm provides insights that can reshape our understanding of diversity and attend to assumptions about mobility, belonging, and difference, then one starting point for this conversation is the very subject of diversity/difference research. In this regard, the subject of research and subjectivity need attention to underscore the fundamentally different assumptions guiding them under a transnational perspective. To address these issues, this chapter delves deeper into issues related to ontological and epistemic assumptions of existing approaches to the study of subjects under conditions of mobility. Here, it should be noted that it is not the broad array of subjects that are the focus of this chapter but rather how mobility reorients the ways in which organizational research has examined diversity and difference in relation to individuals. It proposes transmigrants as a way to rethink the subjects of work and, in doing so, provides opportunities for rethinking diversity. Another important consideration is the context for studying such new subjectivities. In this sense, the formations of new selves are by themselves not necessarily celebratory or emancipatory moments but they can potentially replicate existing or even create new inequalities across transnational social fields. This issue is taken up more concretely in Chapter 7.

In all, this chapter offers three points. First, the argument presented herein is that the focus on individuals and diversity has generally taken shape under the umbrella concept of 'identity' in the MOS literature and become the predominant way in which scholarship attending to people, culture, and difference understands its subject of study in the context of work and organizations. Such an argument warrants examination of not only the analytic focus of extant literature on diversity and difference but also its fundamental ontological and epistemological assumptions.

While some of the discussions presented here have been considered by Özkazanç-Pan and Calás (2015), here the consideration is to underscore why these approaches are insufficient in examining the transnational aspects of lived experiences in the context of inequalities.

Moving from this critique, the chapter then delves into the first of the emergent subjectivities under consideration in this book, namely that of transmigrants. The discussion focuses on subject formation as an alternative way to theorize people and difference but in a manner that moves it beyond extant critical work in postmodern and poststructuralist tradition. In other words, transmigrants is not a conceptual extension of critical perspectives on identity formation but rather an epistemic engagement with the dynamic ways of being and belonging that emerge in transnational social fields. In this sense, different transnational social fields and scales challenge even relational and processual notions of identity, moving them into spaces and fields that are hitherto undertheorized. Transmigrants speaks to those transcalar social, cultural, and political engagements that are undertaken by people whose movement from one context to another bring about opportunity to continue community memberships, political affiliations, social belonging, or religious practices; for example, the Deutschkei or how Turkey becomes remade in Germany (Argun, 2017) inclusive of transformations in the politics and practice of Islam (Ehrkamp, 2016). In a new context, ways of being and belonging to existing communities of identity and practice may undergo a range of transformations—as such, transmigrants speaks to those transformations in self that accompany mobility.

The final and third section of this chapter focuses on the consequences of theorizing transmigrants for the study of organizations and society more broadly. What impact does theorizing difference through the notion of transmigrants have on scholarly research in/about diversity in management and organization studies? In answering this question, the chapter proposes that the world needs new theories and concepts to speak to and examine the conditions of life, habits of choice and force that are taking shape under globalized neoliberalism. Transnational migration studies offers a 'new language' or theoretical framework and provides new ways to understand the nature and location of society. These insights, in turn, provide alternative theoretical possibilities for our understanding of people, difference, and work through the societal flux.

On critique and identity

Following the critical turn in the social sciences, theories arriving from postmodern and poststructuralist traditions have opened up epistemological spaces and possibilities related to how we produce knowledge about the social world. In organization studies, these critical approaches have fostered conversations around the nature and form of knowledge produced about the social world (Calás and Smircich, 1999, 2018; see also Scheele et al., 2018). As a result, there has been a growing critique of the diversity field by scholars adopting critical approaches that question extant assumptions and epistemological claims. These have included the critical perspectives of postmodernity as well as growing interest and deployment of postcolonial scholarship, critical race theories, queer perspectives, and many others. Within this vein, scholars have raised concerns over instrumental approaches to diversity research that have become decoupled from historical facts and socio-political movements. Diversity research has become depoliticized while the subject of diversity research has become disembodied and apolitical.

An important voice in this critical perspective has been the work of Nkomo (1992), who suggests that diversity research needs to attend to race as an organizing principle of US society and that scholars must use it as an analytic lens to uncover organizational experiences. Similarly, in their seminal compilation, Prasad et al. (1997) focus on marginalized Others and the 'shadow side' of diversity (inequality, marginalization) by assembling work arriving from postcolonial, feminist, realism, discourse theory, and other critical traditions. By doing so, they challenge dominant discourses of diversity and allow consideration for new theorizing and theories to emerge. These concerns are expanded on further by others who are explicit about the relationship between diversity and inequality while including voices that have hitherto been missing from the field (Lorbiecki and Jack, 2000; Konrad, Prasad and Pringle, 2006; Zanoni et al., 2010; Kirton and Greene, 2015).

Focusing specifically on inequality, critical scholars have addressed how hierarchies are replicated in organizations across race (Bell et al., 2014), class (Berrey, 2014; Zanoni et al., 2010) and other dimensions of difference (Berry and Bell, 2012; Bleijenbergh and Fielden, 2015) while suggesting that inclusion of marginalized groups requires an alternative way of organizing and performative activities (Janssens and Zanoni, 2014). Others have called for organizational reflection to open up possibilities for agency in the face of dominant assimilation discourses of cultural Others (Ghorashi and Ponzoni, 2014). Reflecting on the lack of meaningful change and progress in organizations for marginalized groups, Prasad et al. (2011) suggest that the adoption of diversity management practices may be fashionable but lack local relevance. The result is diversity management or, as pointed out by these critical scholars, a set of trendy, isomorphic practices aimed to encourage more women and minorities to be part of the organization. Yet such practices may not be relevant or even effective in the local context in which they are supposed to make a difference. Further yet, they may even create a token status in individuals who are hired as the 'face of diversity' such that the impetus and location of change becomes located in particular people rather than in the structures of the organization.

To this end, Ahmed (2007a, 2007b) suggests that diversity has become a non-performance such that the act of documenting diversity has become a substitute for doing diversity. More radically, Jacques (2015) suggests that the critical turn in diversity research has already been mainstreamed and that much of the promise it once held in destabilizing managerialist approaches has vanished. In contrast, other scholars suggest that gender mainstreaming may remediate inequality as biases based on gender are voiced and challenged in organizational settings (Benschop and Verloo, 2006; Van den Brink et al., 2010). Focusing explicitly on the actual practices associated with diversity, such as training, mentoring, and networking, Benschop et al. (2015) state mainstream diversity management approaches can potentially address inequality if they are structured with specific content and formats directed at participants. In other words, the content and form of diversity management matters. In all, these approaches bring about important critique focusing on particular practices, voices, and approaches related to diversity both as a concept and a set of practices. Beyond these critiques, there are examples and instances of identity becoming an important aspect of theorizing and research on/about diversity and difference.

Within management and organization studies, an important and growing stream of critical work focuses specifically on identities. This body of critical scholarly work adopts various theoretical and intellectual traditions to voice alternatives to mainstream diversity research. Some of the critique focuses on mainstream approaches and their focus on only one diversity dimension at a time, such as gender, race or ability. Other critical perspectives in relation to identity focus on subjects. For example, in bringing queer theory to bear on diversity research, scholars illuminate how heteronormative assumptions guide much of the research on identities and offer redirections for diversity research in organizations (Bendl et al., 2008, 2009). Focusing on alternative ways to conceptualize subjects that go beyond static or one dimensional notions of self, scholars have used narrative approaches to identity formation (Van Laer and Janssens, 2014) and called for an intersectional approach to theorizing identities in organizations (Özbilgin et al., 2011; Tatli and Özbilgin, 2012; Atewologun et al., 2015). Critical theories and processual methods are used to defy identity categories and demonstrate the complex and relational nature of identities while, at the same time, expanding diversity research beyond reified categories of gender and race.

One powerful example is through intersectionality, a concept coined by Crenshaw (1991), which allows careful examination of how inequalities take shape at the intersections of gender, race, class, and other relations of power (Collins, 1998; Brah and Phoenix, 2004; McCall, 2005; Yuval-Davis, 2006; Davis, 2008). By mapping out the complex relationship between societal norms, organizational structures, and the intersecting dimensions of difference, this approach has yielded important insights about the experiences of women of color in workplaces and organizations (Holvino, 2010). As a conceptual framework, intersectionality has allowed for rethinking the interplay between privilege and oppression to enact change (Rodriguez et al., 2016) in work contexts.

Altogether, critical approaches allow consideration for the relational and multi-layered ways in which people relate to others, experience privilege and oppression, and enact and form identities within work and organizational contexts. Through their varied theoretical insights, critical work provides much needed voice to important topics generally not considered by most diversity scholars. In all, these approaches represent attempts to complicate conceptualizations of difference, or the ways people can be differentiated from each other and theorized beyond existing identity label and categories. Despite these aspirations, such diversity research continues to use identity despite its meta-theoretical foundations in Western individualism and psychological constructs (Özkazanç-Pan and Calás, 2015). In effect, identity categories cannot be deployed without recognizing their historic and epistemic foundations and, thus, going beyond 'post-identitarian' approaches to theorizing difference and selves in the context of globalization and migration requires engagement with mobile subjectivity or those *ways of being* and *ways of belonging* (Levitt and Glick Schiller, 2004) that traverse time, space and sites in a multiscalar fashion. New frameworks are necessary to (re)consider the subjects of diversity management as ideas, people, and practices travels across borders and boundaries.

To clarify, while subjectivity can be understood as the emergent and relational embodied subject arising from discursive, textual, and material practices (Rose, 2009), mobile subjectivity focuses on the agentic possibilities associated with *ways of being and belonging* in the everyday lives and experiences of people with histories of migration. As Archer (2007: 22) suggests in considering the relationship between structure and agency, 'the examination of agential subjectivity and reflexive variability become even more important in order to understand differences of response under the same ("unacknowledged") conditions'. In other words, people engage in *reflexive deliberation* to *subjectively* determine their actions in relation to the *objective* situation in which they are embedded (Archer, 2007: 28).

In this sense, attending to *mobile* subjectivities requires attending to how and why people engage in particular activities in order to understand the construction of selves. This approach stands in stark contrast to the use of identity categories to reflect differences that already exist in contrast to an understanding of how selves and difference are accomplished in a multiscalar fashion. In other words, mobile subjectivities require constant accomplishing to be in existence. It is in this agentic and reflexive practice of accomplishing or *ways of being and belonging* that transnational migration studies provides new notions of self that eschew nation-based or static identity-based concepts of self and notions of difference no matter their critical epistemologies. A transnational approach decolonizes hierarchical conceptualizations of identity and opens up opportunities for theorizing difference and subject formation beyond multi-identity approaches (such as bi-national, bi-racial, or multicultural). As exemplars of these new possible selves and the ways in which they embody and engage in social, cultural, economic, and political activities, *transmigrants* speaks to new possibilities of personhood arising from the embedded nature of people across scales as they actively construct and reconstruct their lives.

Transmigrants

Transmigrants can be defined as people whose sense of self is derived from their mobile experiences and active engagement within socio-cultural, economic and/or political realms that span scales. Such individuals may hold citizenship in at least two or more nation-states. However, rather than limit our understanding of transmigrants to legal status or citizenship, it is important to note that by way of technology, communities of practice and belonging can materialize across boundaries and scales. In such instances, transmigrants can materialize not due to their ability to cross nation-state borders or have multiple citizenship rights but with respect to how they make meaning of their lives and undertake agentic ways of understanding of themselves. This clarification is important given that nation-states are a problematic unit for understanding and defining mobility—a point that is expanded on in Chapter 8 in relation to mobile methodologies.

In recent years, examples of why this clarification is important have become more poignant given that nations are built through epistemic (Bhabha, 1990), material and legal practices, such as integration policies (Shore, 2013; Joppke and Morawska, 2014). In other words, declaring a piece of land as a particular nation-state requires conversations around history, race/ethnicity, and violence: certain groups and their histories are rendered invisible in order to create a linear, purified narrative of modern nationhood (Latour, 2012). The notion of transmigrants addresses these points rather than becoming beholden to the idea of the bounded, physical nation-state as the only foundation for theorizing mobility. Consequently, transmigrants as an analytic concept attends to those lived experiences of transnationalism and lives across social fields even if the person in question is not able or allowed to cross physical nation-state borders. As an example, the plight of people who were 'illegally' brought to the US as children continues to surface in contemporary debates around the status of such individuals and their 'rights' in a liberal democracy. Such discussions bring to bear questions around how nations are defined inclusive of who is considered as belonging to it and who is consider an immigrant.

In the US, this issue is rarely addressed and, when it is, political partisanship coupled with racist, alt-right ideologies have become de facto rhetoric in these past few years. There is little discussion around the existence of First Nations who inhabited and continue to inhabit, albeit in few numbers, the North American continent centuries prior to the arrival of Europeans. Historically, the lack of discussion around immigration as it relates to Indigenous people/nations and land rights in the US in contrast to Canada, New Zealand and even Australia has created increased contemporary tensions around race/ethnicity and belonging (Scholtz, 2013). To clarify, the starting point for history in the US is the arrival of Western Europeans rather than any other moment in time—as a consequence, the US is deemed a nation of brave, freedom-seekers fleeing from imperial British control rather than a nation forged through genocide and slavery. Yet this is essentially White, settler history and the lack of recognition of the violent consequences of their migration is not theorized in contemporary conversations around what it means to be an American.

In this sense, the historic and forceful taking of land to create a nation requires discussion about (im)migration, politics, economic structures, and the social imaginary of nationhood. Unfortunately, these historic elements, which are highly relevant for contemporary conversations around diversity and 'identity', are not considered in theories about difference. This is true even in instances whereby the particular notion of difference arrives from critical epistemologies as even such work tends to focus on identity rather than history as well as socio-economic and political structures that have led to the production of the very concepts of race/ethnicity and culture. Without attending to these issues, any theories of diversity, difference, and belonging can inevitably become about identity even if they tend to focus on multiple iterations of identities. Diversity literature has its foundations in the US and, hence, the lack of historical context in most work, with notable exceptions (such as the work of Nkomo) in contemporary diversity research, can be traced back to the ways in which the subject was formulated and studied in business schools.

The approach to people, culture, and difference in the management literature does not necessarily draw on transnational lenses or even critical work in most cases. By limiting the kinds of theories that are used to study and conceptualize diversity, extant MOS work provides narrow ideas around why and how people may have different understandings of themselves and their lives. Issues of agency, reflexivity, and history become vacated in favor of identity research. Yet this is fundamentally a short-sighted enterprise in the search for understanding of why and how people craft their personal and professional lives in particular ways. This limited view is then extended to the study of work and organizations as such sites are assumed to be where 'diverse identities' have encounters, resulting in potential conflict and other organizational outcomes (as identified in Chapter 1). Yet there is much more complexity around society and nationhood that warrants attention in any theories which aim to speak about 'diversity' in the context of work and organizations.

To this end, transmigrants as a framework focuses on the making of transnational lives and, in doing so, reflects a kind of agentic, reflexive subjectivity with limits around possibilities—as certain groups of people have opportunities to create lives and livelihoods while others do not and that certain groups have recognized histories and lands, while others do not (such as Kurds, Indigenous groups). More than this, transmigrants speaks to the past, present, and possible future as it incorporates not only agentic, reflexive notions of self but also considerations of history and relations between/among different nations (rather than nation-states) as a starting point for new imaginaries of self and society.

The key focus herein is the notion of agency and its limits within the context of new formations of society and nation-rebuilding across transnational social fields. Transmigrants speak simultaneously to lived agentic experiences of self as well as those histories which underscore contemporary work lives. As an example, Ehrkamp (2005) examines the transformation of German neighborhoods by Turkish immigrants with transnational social ties. These ties are then manifest through their material organizational practices (creating community centers and mosques) and social engagements (mass media). The study points out that such multiscalar activities produce transmigrant selves embedded in local 'German' neighborhoods but at the same time pivoting toward Turkey based on notions of who Turkish immigrants are in the historic context of Germany. These narratives of belonging focus on ethnicity, labor force participation and citizenship, and engagement in political activities in Germany *and* in Turkey. This example highlights that the intersections of work and organizational life are very much influenced by agentic practices—in other words, the ethnic labor of Turkish transmigrants in Germany is not simply a matter of 'diverse identities at work' but rather a conversation about historic narratives of arrival and contemporary practices of nation-rebuilding and belonging. The ways in which these narratives and practices take shape in work and organizational contexts cannot be seen or captured by focusing on identities. Rather, transmigrant speaks to those broader, scalar, and agentic practices that individuals and communities develop as a means to shape their lives and experiences.

The engagement of such groups in certain activities and not others signals both agency and a reflexive stance as they aim to define and structure the conditions under which they want to be in Germany, at least on a local level. These acts inevitably involve workplaces and organizations, such as community centers and mosques in the example above, in order to transpire. Thus, attending to workplaces and other forms of organizations simply as containers of diverse people is insufficient for understanding the socio-cultural, racial/ethnic and political dimensions of such spaces in sustaining transnational communities. In this sense, work is not necessarily the context for homo economicus and related to conversations around productivity and contributions *despite* the diversity of participants. Rather, workplaces are considered sites of encounters between different people, narratives of society and belonging, and socio-political engagements. Any resulting tension then is not necessarily due to 'diverse identities' but the fact that particular narratives of nation, race/ethnicity, and belonging are foundational for how workplaces are organized and embodied. Such assumptions come to surface when they are challenged by groups who 'transgress' or enter those spaces and places which were, until their arrival, not for them—this is fundamentally about difference (race/ethnicity and migration histories) and belonging and, hence, a new way to think about how diversity is framed beyond issues of identity. If diversity is the name we give transgressions into workplaces and organizations of dominant groups, then transmigrants expands this concept to include narratives of nation, transnational social lives, and ranges of scales.

Transmigrants forces scholars to rethink workplaces and organizations as sites and spaces beyond the boundaries put on them by narratives of business (such as functional units, coordination, control, profit logic). Workplaces embody different kinds of transnational communities, which materialize through the social interactions, material practices, and symbolic constructions of its members (Djelic and Quack, 2010). Consequently, transnational communities and selves are not necessarily bound together by physical proximity or territory as in nations but rather through 'imagined' and agentic ways of belonging (Anderson, 2006) across time, space, and sites. In turn, organizations including workplaces represent transnational social spaces (Pries, 2001, 2008) and sites, and are a part of broader transnational community-building practices that people engage in. To this end, Islam (2013) suggests that encounters between migrants and natives in 'shared spaces', such as workplaces and other organizations, offers new discussions around locality beyond binaries, such as citizen/noncitizen or migrant/native.

Transmigrant as a conceptual lens to study the complexity of lives stands in stark contrast to the approach adopted for study of people who traverse between cultures, another approach to the study of diversity in a global context. The hallmark of MOS and cross-cultural management research is the study of bi-cultural and multicultural individuals. While these identity categories recognize that people may share values and ways of being in the world that are associated with more than one culture, the epistemology of such work derives from psychological schema research. This research aims to outline how individuals develop (multi)cultural schemas (Fitzsimmons, 2013) or multicultural personalities (Leone et al., 2005). To clarify, bi- or multicultural individuals are thoughts to have 'internalized more than one set of cultural schemas' where schema is understood as a 'socially constructed cognitive system that represents one's knowledge about the values, attitudes, beliefs, and behavioral assumptions of a culture' (Brannen and Thomas, 2010: 6; see also Fiske and Taylor, 2013). Identity then derives from such cultural schemas and provides ways for researchers to understand the coping mechanisms of bi- or multicultural individuals in relation to different contexts. Again, the impetus for such research is the impact of (psycho-social) culture on identity and how, in turn, these different identities impact workplaces.

For management scholars, the overarching concern is to find ways that these individuals can contribute to the competitive advantage of organizations that are operating in complex and everchanging environments as per globalization (Brannen and Thomas, 2010). Thus, adopting such a diversity/difference lens to conceptualize people and study how they make sense of the world significantly limits the transnational ways of being and belonging that take shape not only through organizational contexts but also in their everyday lives. Agency, reflexivity and mobility, hallmark considerations of transnational migration studies, call attention to the ways in which people assemble their sense of self in a multiscalar fashion. This assembling of selves reflects an agentic and reflexive epistemology whereby axioms of culture become delinked from their epistemological foundations in Western psychological constructs (Okazaki et al., 2008).

Such subjectivities represent simultaneously the unmooring of psychology from its Cartesian dualism (consciousness related to separation of mind and body) and the re-inscription of it as an embodied multiscalar process through which people make sense of themselves and the world. The assembling of selves in this fashion reflects historic colonial relations and other relations of power whereby particular groups of people were subjugated as significant to the production of selves and formation of subjectivities.

Snel et al. (2006) complicate further these points on agentic subjectivities by addressing the relevance of history *and* neoliberalism in their accomplishment. Specifically, they outline how different sets of transmigrant groups, such as those from Japan, US, Morocco and Iraq in the Netherlands, enact subjectivities through socio-cultural and economic activities based on their specific historic experiences in terms of race, ethnicity, and labor position. These issues take place within the historic context of 'guest workers' in Europe and elsewhere, a legacy of capitalist expansion under globalization whereby industrialized nations require low-wage workers from transition or developing nations for their growing economies (Hahamovitch, 2003). These trends continue in the present day and have contributed to ongoing debates in Europe's liberal nations on ways to 'assimilate' or integrate cultural Others (Koopmans, 2005), a discussion that is echoed in the US through discourses of 'managing diversity/diversity management' (Albrecht, 2001). The remaking of America (and other nations) via immigration (Alba and Nee, 2009) requires attending to the ways institutions and organizations might be changing (Karraker, 2013) through neoliberalism and migration. Within this context, the economic and political structuring of societies coupled with dominant cultural narratives of the nation (Bhabha, 1990) can produce limits on the kinds of agency and reflexive action possible by such transnational selves. Nonetheless, these studies demonstrate that people undertake action that redefines the conditions of possibility for their families, work, and communities.

In all, the way of being and belonging enacted in an agentic fashion by transmigrants remakes the organizations, communities, and neighborhoods that they inhabit but, as importantly, these activities also remake societies and nations: what does it mean to be a citizen of a particular nation? The narratives, practices, and potential struggles of transmigrants challenge the boundaries of nations (Ehrkamp and Leitner, 2006) and the possibility of a 'national culture': an epistemic stronghold in much of the literature in cross-cultural management. In contrast, notions of flexible citizenship (Ong, 1999) and partial citizenship (Parrenas, 2001) available from a transnational lens speak to the challenges of workers that move between and among nations. On this point, Parrenas (2001) observes that in the case of Filipina domestic workers, one of the largest contingent of transmigrant workers globally, many labor and workplace protections afforded citizens are not available, resulting in excessive work hours, sexual harassment and abuse, little to no overtime pay, and physical confinement in the home of the employers. As such, mobile subjectivities and a transmigrant framework have much to offer in rethinking how nation and culture are deployed in conceptualizing possibilities for work experiences, values, and behaviors across global organizational contexts given that such experiences and actions are not sufficiently seen or theorized through the axioms of diversity research given the focus on identity and culture as categories of identification.

New approaches to theorizing work?

In many ways, transmigrants, as a conceptual framework speaking to reflexive, agentic subjectivity, provides new opportunities for rethinking and retheorizing work and organizations broadly. First, rather than seeing work as a bounded organization where one earns a living, this approach reimagines work as a series of encounters between/among different people in relation to narratives of nationhood and belonging. This new idea promotes a dynamic understanding of work that moves it beyond a static space to an interactive one. In contrast, diverse identities as a lens to understand such experiences and encounters cannot account for the agentic nature of subjectivities and their transnational practices. If we reimagine work from the lens of transmigrants, then new opportunities arise for understanding how and why certain tensions may be taking shape in the organization. Such tensions are not necessarily the product of cultural differences or diversity but rather emanate from fundamentally different lived experiences of belonging, race/ethnicity, and nation-building practices.

If nation-states are the products of dominance of particular people and ideas over others, then contemporary workplaces and organizations need to be understood within this historic context. Rather than only focusing on neoliberalism as a growing and global form of economic arrangement, the historic and contemporary forms of migration and mobility that continue to take shape must also be recognized. Narratives of becoming and belonging as they relate to one's position in and relation to society are important considerations in understanding work experiences in addition to neoliberalism. As the examples in this chapter demonstrate, work experiences cannot be theorized only within the boundaries of one organization. Rather, there must be an emphasis and consideration of the very nature of society and how people engage in particular social, political, and cultural activities of a transnational nature. This is the case for people with and without migratory histories given that technology has enabled new possibilities for engaging with communities, ideas, and places across the globe. Whether these take shape in relation to political activism, social causes, or even cultural consumptions, such as movies, transnational social fields broadly and transmigrants specifically speak to these new subjectivities.

In all, transmigrants proposes that workplaces and organizational contexts are not containers of different kinds of people but sites and spaces whereby particular narratives of nationhood, experiences of belonging, and agentic practices come to take shape. Consequently, the study of work experiences, workplaces, and organizations broadly must attend to societal and historic context. Mobility as a guiding ontological condition remakes contemporary subjectivities, moving them out of the defined boundaries of diversity and culture research in MOS. Rather, the focus is shifted from static forms of identification and their relevance for work experiences and organization outcomes to a historic, transnational one which recognizes society, history and social fields as relevant to theorizing organizations. This recognition of mobility and transmigrants as a new subject of work requires a fundamental shift in how management and organization studies understands the subject of study and acknowledges the contexts that impact lived experiences, agentic practices, and reflexive formations of self. Through this shift and by using a transnational migration studies theoretical lens, MOS scholars can begin to understand the complexity of experiences in workplaces and other forms of organizations beyond identity categories and cultural schemas.

4

Hybrid Selves

In this chapter, the focus is on hybrids as another form of subjectivity taking shape under conditions of mobility. The previous chapter focused on transmigrants, emphasizing the agentic and reflexive nature of transnational selves that are formed with particular attention to issues of belonging, nationhood, and race/ethnicity. The emphasis herein is on the creation of novel ways of being and belonging to the social world that take shape through transnational scales. The added element beyond the agentic and reflexive consideration of the previous chapter is the creative, emergent, and novel aspects of subjectivity that take shape depending on context and encounters. These new hybrid subjectivities are not readily represented by the axioms of diversity and difference research as they use problematic notions of identity and culture as the main frameworks. Notably, such subjectivities arrive out of the intersections of three important considerations: the epistemic, social, and material dimensions as understood from a transnational lens. Hence, this chapter focuses on those elements that make hybrid selves the new subjects of work and, in doing so, provides alternative ways for theorizing and studying subjectivities arriving out of mobility ontologies. To achieve this, the first section provides an outline of what constitutes hybrid selves followed by how such subjectivities manifest themselves at work through empirical examples. In the third and final section, there is discussion of the epistemic, social, and material dimensions that altogether allow for the emergence of hybrid selves with implications around how differences are studied and valued in MOS.

Understanding hybrids

Hybrid selves and hybridity more broadly is an approach to understanding in-between, third space subjectivities that arise from the encounters between/among different people and cultures, where culture is understood as a shifting set of scripts, narratives, and sense of the world. As a concept that speaks to liminal spaces, hybridity also has currency in postcolonial traditions (Young, 1995/2005; Frenkel and Shenhav, 2006; Özkazanç-Pan, 2008), in literature (Bakhtin, 1981) and in work that speaks to the intersections of feminism and cultural studies (Anzaldúa, 1987; Saldívar-Hull, 2000). In postcolonial traditions, hybridity speaks to those agentic colonizer–colonized encounters whereby the rules of recognition were being defied, including attempts to subvert colonial authority (Fanon, 1952/2008, 1963; Bhabha, 1990). In the work of Bakhtin (1977, 1981), the analysis engages hybrid uses of language and ways in which hybridity shapes the social and political imaginary.

In work that has attended to mixings through a feminist and cultural studies perspectives, the focus has been on the emergence of *mestiza* or the formation of hybrid consciousness that arises as people start creating and occupying 'borderlands' in claiming elements from different cultures. This is most prominent in the work of Chicana feminist Gloria Anzaldúa as she speaks to those epistemic formations that open up spaces for becoming and writing a novel kind of subjectivity beyond dominant paradigms in (Western) literature. By opening up the possibility of writing differently, her work speaks to the emergence of transgressive subjectivities arising as hybrids rather than pure, bounded literary figures. This is different than other attempts to speak about being 'Other', such as W.E.B. DuBois (1903, 1940) and his concepts of the 'veil' and 'double consciousness' from his research into Black communities at the turn of the 20th century. Or similarly, Audre Lorde's 'Sister Outsider' (1984) speaks to the experiences of marginalized people and cultures in the US from a position of Black, feminist, and queer positionality.

In all, these various theoretical engagements bring together dimensions of race/ethnicity, belonging, and difference and are important examinations of experiences, processes, and practices related to nationhood and subjectivities. Building on these rich and important works that theorize and examine hybridity, the notion of hybridity noted in this book focuses on the consequences of transnational encounters, ranging from the physical to the virtual. Here, the focus is on hybrid as a conceptual tool and subjectivity that speaks to those new and emergent ways of being and belonging arriving out of the intersections of epistemic, social, and material practices. In most simple terms, it is a way to understand how people may draw from different and even paradoxical practices derived from the various communities with which they identify. Yet the concepts arriving out of such frameworks do not address or examine the transnational modes through which hybrid selves are derived in an agentic and reflexive fashion. Consequently, the contemporary ways in which individuals emerge as hybrids cannot be captured by the extant theoretical frameworks of even these critical perspectives. Hybrids take shape not only in terms of their current location and in a dialectic manner but in a transnational fashion that allows blending of selves, ideas, and practices across scales—such as religious practices, political ideologies, cultural goods, and social tastes. Altogether, the simultaneous epistemic, social, and material dimensions in a transnational mode separate a transnational understanding and influence on hybridity compared to these existing approaches arriving out of different traditions: postcolonial, literary theory, feminisms, cultural studies, and critical race perspectives.

While this chapter builds on these critical traditions in offering another perspective in conceptualizing hybridity, the critique is focused explicitly on MOS literature that also claims to examine 'difference'. That is, the chapter offers a critical understanding of MOS work while at the same offering alternative ways to consider the subjects of work through the subjectivity of hybridity. At its most immediate, hybrid challenges conceptualizations of 'self' based on the epistemic finality of identity categories no matter their relational, processual (Schultz et al., 2012), or intersectional nature (Holvino, 2010). In other words, hybrid signifies a new kind of self that arises as a result of the distinct context, experiences, and set of social and material practices that a person engages in to understand themselves and those around them. While there are several different ways to define hybrid, here I deploy it specifically as those novel socio-cultural transformations, combinations, and 'mixings' that take shape at the moment of cultural encounter (Kalra et al., 2005). These mixings are conceptualized specifically in relation to those epistemic, social, and material ways of being and belonging that contribute to the emergence of hybrid subjectivity. That is, while extant identity categories offer boundaries around how people can be identified and differentiated, hybrid challenges those boundaries. It does so in several ways.

First, the idea of hybrids reflects the ways in which there is agency and reflexivity in how people choose to craft selves—this means that rather than only differentiating oneself in terms that are available from local narratives, people can rely on transnational modes and communities as a means of relating their lives to the lives of people who may not be co-located. While the agentic and reflexive nature of subjectivity was outlined in the previous chapter on transmigrants, here the focus is on the emergent and novel ways subjectivities emerge via mixings. By drawing on stories, communities, and practices of people who are beyond the immediate context, hybridity allows consideration of the ways in which subjectivities are forged across space and place. Cultural encounters can take shape not only in the immediate physical context of one's work, neighborhood, community, or nation but also across transnational scales.

Extending further on this point, hybrid selves form differently even if facing the same set of circumstances and conditions—studying the everyday lives of people can elucidate the repertoires of actions that they embody and eschew (Ley, 2004). In this sense, there are no formulas for understanding whether particular hybrids will emerge. Rather, it is relevant to consider how in-between, novel mixings (Anzaldúa, 1987) contribute to the emergence of hybrids including those taking shape within workplaces and in/across different organizations (Gutiérrez et al., 1999). If hybridity is the new norm to understand subjects at work, then questions around how we voice and value differences is also required: in diversity and cross-cultural management research, particular kinds of differences are voiced and researched while others become ignored. Transnational migration studies and the conceptual framework derived from key conversations in the field can expand the concepts available to study people, hybridity being one of these new subjects which specifically eschews boundary- and category-based approaches.

Second, the notion of cultural encounters is expanded beyond the confines of cultural schemas as the dominant way in which culture is generally defined in the MOS field. Cultural schema as a concept emphasizes shared values, norms, and habits of the mind. Rather, the consideration from a transnational migration perspective is beyond the immediate encounter between different cultures and people. It includes the historic context of the encounter and the ongoing transnational modes that allow additional encounters to take shape. The initial encounter and ensuing additional encounters exemplify a challenge to potentially long held beliefs around who or what constitutes the nation. It necessitates a re-examination of the ways in which culture and cultural understandings of people are derived from particular assumptions about race/ethnicity and nationhood. Hybridity opens up possibilities for ways of being and belonging to the social world that are simultaneously rooted in particular local contexts but also shift across transnational scales. In doing so, it challenges the replication of homogenous or static ideas around who belongs to a particular nation-state and, consequently, who is considered an outsider. It does so by focusing attention on the fact that claiming a particular subjectivity is not being someone else or belonging in some other way.

For example, to suggest someone is *Asian*-American is more than a practice of identification: it is also a conversation about the fact that diversity and cross-cultural management research do not acknowledge how arrivals, encounters, and agency impact subjectivities. In other words, if *Asian* is simply seen as a qualifier for American, then there is little consideration of what constitutes American or how that in turn impacts Asian. The in-between possibilities are currently bridged by a simple hyphen despite the complexity associated with being and belonging as both processes and practices. Not all iterations of Asian-American look the same and, thus, this blended identity cannot serve as a conceptual framework that can represent all the various ways Asian and American can mix. The hyphen then is the most powerful signifier in this assembly of cultural and national categories but perhaps it is also the most overlooked. Rather than assuming that all hyphenations represent the same acculturation process and attendant epistemic, social, and material practices, hybridity opens up opportunities to study the different ways hyphenation takes shape.

Finally, hybridity signifies new possibilities for understanding the role of context. Context becomes an important and differentiating factor in how hybrid selves come to form and impact possibilities of self—already, there are examinations of such hybridity from a migration perspective (Papastergiadis, 2018), but here the focus is on the transnational elements of hybridity. In other words, hybridity can be the coming together of different mixings by drawing up different elements and scales in a transnational manner. This stands in contrast to culture-based concepts of identity that seemingly do not allow examination of how people may draw on different spheres to craft their subjectivities. Culture as exemplified in MOS does not allow consideration for the dynamic nature of selves beyond bi-culturals and multiculturalism as a container for people who may identify with more than one culture. Ultimately, there is a difference between identification and agentic, reflexive engagement. The former assumes that culture is a given and people may choose to identify with it or not. The latter suggests that culture is created and novel forms of it may be possible particularly through the ongoing encounters of people and their histories in a transnational manner.

In all, these points speak to the elements of hybridity that attend to issues of agency, reflexivity, and novelty—that is, hybridity speaks to those creative and novel ways in which people can invent and reinvent themselves across contexts. In doing so, they challenge extant theories that would put boundaries around culture and identity in order to demarcate where one kind of person or culture ends and another starts. In other words, what is an African-American, an Afro-Latinx, British-of-South East Asian descent, Iraqi-Kurd, or any other abbreviated appellation? Similarly, notions of *hapa* as derived from imperial encounters in Hawaii (Bernstein and De la Cruz, 2009) and *hakka* as references to indigenous communities in 'multicultural' Taiwan (Wang, 2007) also speak to these cultural and racial mixings in history and in contemporary context. In all, there is little examination of these complex and new combinations that have taken shape due to colonization, imperial conquests, and other encounters, including their current continuation in contemporary lives in much of MOS literature. In the next section, examples of work that speak to hybridity are shared as they relate to work and organizational contexts. By focusing on how hybrids materialize in workplaces and organizational contexts, the goal is to demonstrate their contributions to rethinking diversity and difference as exemplified in the MOS field.

Hybrids at work

As one example of a focused study on hybrids, Leonard (2010) uses such an approach to expose how 'organizing Whiteness' in postcolonial Hong Kong takes place through subject formation efforts of 'expatriates' across relations of gender and nationality. Her work exemplifies the use of different scales and historic conjunctures to understand how power and privilege play out in organizational contexts in contrast to adopting a comparative approach that might, for example, aim to distinguish between foreigners/expatriates and native-born employees on various psychological, social or cultural dimensions of diversity. As a point of contrast, Leonard's (2010) use of Whiteness as a lens is substantively different than a similar study by Steyn (2005) who examines Whiteness and 'White talk' to construct transnational selves among White South Africans in South Africa and in the diaspora.

Both studies focus on notions of Whiteness as they relate to the formation of hybrid subjectivities but, in each case, the research attends to the specificity of the socio-cultural, historical, political, and economic context that contributes uniquely to the production of such selves. These studies demonstrate that Whiteness is a specific hybrid subjectivity that emerges differently and that there is little conceptual 'sameness' between the terms. In other words, the conceptual framework available from diversity research would posit a multicultural identity framework to study such individuals but in doing so, would not be able to attend to the specificity of subjectivity and the *ways of belonging* that are embodied in the notion of Whiteness in each circumstance.

Understood within the context of transnational migration, hybridity posits that the reflexive embodiment of a particular notion of self is not equivalent across all people such that being Black in the US, Jamaican-British, Chinese-Malay, or Turkish-German among many other ways of becoming are not the same: in the same context; and across different contexts through the multiscalar networks and practices adopted by people. Hyphenation as a psychological process, and social practice of hybridization represents a blending of transnational selves (Asher, 2008) and requires constant accomplishing in the context of migration and postcoloniality as conditions of history (Bhatia and Ram, 2009). Such notions of self are further complicated by ways of being and belonging that derive subjectivity through references to diaspora experiences (Bhatia, 2012) whereby physical travel no longer becomes necessary for the construction of transnational selves and lives (Blunt, 2007).

As an example of these points, Dwyer (2000) focuses on how 'young British South Asian Muslim women' construct hybrid selves by simultaneously adopting and challenging pan-Islamic discourses of religion, gender norms in the UK and in their families, racialization of postcolonial immigrants from South Asia and changes in the local labor market that resulted in increased opportunities for clerical and service work in contrast to the manual labor work available for their male family members. Such selves take shape through specific narratives that reference the historic ways such women and their families came to the UK from a former British colony and position 'Pakistan' as the authority for matters of Islamic morality and piety. Within the US context, Mishra and Shirazi (2010) focus on American Muslim women with immigrant backgrounds and their experiences in the US post-9/11 in relation to the *hijab* or the Muslim veil/head covering. The scholars examine the production of local hybrid selves as American, Muslim, and women in the context of broader global discourses related to Islamic fundamentalism, female modesty in Islam, and 'being American'. Their interviews outline how such women identify themselves as American Muslimah (Muslim women) through individualized enactments of Islam that include different narratives around their decision to wear or not wear the *hijab* in public and in work contexts and the potential transnational consequences (such as shame) of (un)veiling for relatives in other nations. These practices are derived from an epistemological engagement with axioms of Islam that are not only local but also come from traditions of different Muslim communities. The social practice associated with veiling is more than a convention but an agentic and reflexive act which is taken up with purpose and intentions in a very particular context: post-9/11 US. Finally, the materiality associated with veiling is a consideration of the very physical and embodied ways such women present themselves. Altogether, the epistemic, social, and material practices associated with veiling speak to the complexity of a transnational hybrid self that emerges in the context of the US.

For Mishra and Shirazi (2010), the everyday veiling practices of such women reflect their simultaneous fight against Islamophobia and

Islamic extremism, and thus are good examples of agentic, reflexive subjectivity whose very existence is both a socio-cultural and political enactment. While this example highlights the ways hybrid selves might take shape, it can be contrasted with two similar studies that also focus on Muslim women and 'identity' but derive their analyses through a priori categories that limit their ability to see the formation of agentic, reflexive subjectivities in transnational social fields. In the context of diversity research, what possibilities exist for voicing the complexity of hybrid selves and the implications of such worldviews for understanding and studying work experiences in organizations and beyond?

To exemplify this point, I expand on and contrast two studies in the MOS field that offer similar subjects of study: Muslim women and the implications of their religious practices, such as veiling, for identity formation. Berger et al. (2017) examine identity construction work by Muslim women of Moroccan descent in Dutch organizations by using the lens of structuration theory and Whiteness to uncover ways human resource management (HRM) practices can be more inclusive. The authors select topics from 'popular discourse' that they consider to be representative of various issues facing Muslims: alcohol and food, Ramadan and holidays, prayers, and wearing a headscarf (Berger et al., 2017: 1127). They then address how Muslim women negotiate their identity in relation to these issues in the context of predominantly White organizations. In a similar study, Syed and Pio (2010) examine Muslim migrant women in Australia through a multi-level perspective focused on macro-societal, meso-organizational and micro-individual dimensions. They focus on the experiences of such women in formal work contexts and suggest that the complex nature of gender, migration, and societal expectations may preclude the ability of organizations to be solely responsible for diversity management. In other words, diversity management may not be a good 'fix' for the issues facing such women in terms of inclusion and work experiences.

Taken together, these two studies represent a point of contrast to the previous two studies that speak of hybrid selves in transnational social field: in the latter two studies, Muslim women is conceptualized as an a priori identity category despite recognition of the migrant histories of the women interviewed for the studies. In the first set of studies related to Muslim women, the complexity of ongoing social, cultural, economic, and political negotiations results in hybrid selves that defy categorization. As a point of contrast, the lenses available from diversity research conceptualize such individuals as 'minority ethnic women in organizations', thereby erasing their history of becoming. Moreover, the positionality of the researchers in 'knowing' their subjects as Muslim in terms of epistemic claims and power relations or what 'difference difference makes' in the context fieldwork (McCorkel and Myers, 2003) are left unexplored.

Despite undertaking a relational understanding of identity formation, there is no consideration of the *ways of being and belonging* of 'Muslim (im)migrant women' such that agency and reflexivity do not become guiding frameworks for the formation of subjectivities. Without recognizing the transnational journey that allows hybrid subjectivities to emerge via socio-cultural, ethnic and religious ways of being and belonging, diversity research is unable to recognize agency on the part of these women to be Muslim, British, or Dutch and women concurrently. As Bhatia and Ram (2001) suggest, Western social psychological constructs assume problematically that all immigrants go through the same psychological acculturation processes whereby the 'universal cognitive self' becomes changed through a cultural encounter. This psychological notion of self and culture also guides diversity research that aims to explain the experiences of bi-/multicultural individuals or, in these cases, ethnic and religious minority women. Culture, as derived from psychological constructs, does not suffice as a lens for differentiating and comparing people given its static ontological basis and epistemic limits.

Finally, both studies prioritize work settings and organizations for the study of identity formation processes. Despite adopting a relational approach, the researchers are not able to examine the transnational and multiscalar nature of such processes beyond the immediate context under study. In other words, even a multi-level analysis, such as the one adopted by Syed and Pio (2010), cannot uncover the complexity of hybrid selves that emerge out of agentic, reflexive enactments of Islam that differ between and among women who identify as Muslim. By using 'Muslim (im)migrant women' as an already existing category of analysis, neither study focuses on how such women understand themselves and construct their subjectivities through socio-cultural practices, political ideologies, religious discourses, and personal narratives of Islam that span time, space, geographies, and social relationships. To this end, hybrid selves open up possibilities for understanding the complexity of selves and the ways in which different sites, spaces, and narratives become deployed for their emergence. They can also provide insights about new work relations that emerge through encounters in the context of organizations when the arrival of cultural Others requires addressing hitherto unvoiced assumptions about them. In all, hybridity complicates the very notions of identity and organizations: what novel work relations might emerge if we conceptualize organizations as transnational social spaces and attend to encounters between/among different people in a multiscalar fashion?

Understanding the elements: epistemic, social and material

In order to understand how and why the analysis of difference and culture available from a hybridity lens differs from diversity research, a focus on epistemic, social and material practices is required. The first of these elements is the epistemic one and related to the ways in which we produce knowledge about race/ethnicity and difference. And further, how we give meaning and value to those differences. As Canclini suggests, there must be a hermeneutic capacity to the concept of hybridity. He states that it is necessary to give the concept of hybridization 'hermeneutical capacity' in order to '[make] it useful for interpreting relations of meaning that are reconstructed through mixing' (Canclini, 1995: xxix) and, consequently, give it explanatory power. This formulation speaks to the ways in which hybridity is more than a random mixing of ideas, practices, and other elements of one's life. Rather, it is also a conversation around how we come to know difference, and the values and meanings we assign those differences.

In the context of diversity research, many of the aims are related to the connections of diversity to organizational performance or outcomes. In some cases, there are comparisons between different groups of people in relation to outcomes but also experiences. Overall, the concern is not related to why MOS has come to value the search for differences of a particular kind as necessary. The epistemic practices of labeling individuals as belonging to demographic or cultural groups do not speak to the broader issues of why differences as manifest in the diversity research have come to dominate the ways in which we theorize subjectivities and experiences. While some of these disciplinary practices can be understood in relation to the history of the field and its struggle for legitimacy and acceptance, contemporary research in diversity can still push the boundaries of what is acceptable and valuable research. To this end, engaging with the epistemological customs of the field and their consequences is necessary in order to change the trajectory of diversity and difference research.

The second focus as it relates to the value of hybridity as a lens is in the domain of the social. While research on diversity tends to focus only on workplaces and organizations, the social domain is much more expansive. Hybridity allows consideration for transnational scales in relation to the social and, in doing so, opens up possibilities for reimagining and theorizing the ways people may craft their sense of self and sense of belonging. Some of this may take shape in organizational contexts but by limiting analysis only to the domain of the bounded organization, scholars cannot travel with their subjects of study: the new subjects of work materialize across transnational scales and, as such, understanding how they challenge the very boundaries of workplaces and organizations is necessary. By doing so, scholars can expand on existing approaches and analysis of workplaces and organizations that rely on bounded people as their unit of analysis. Rather, by expanding the possibilities for subjectivity in the social domain, scholars can rethink workplaces as sites of encounter between different transnational social communities. Hybridity speaks to these encounters and reimagines workplaces as spaces and sites that change depending on who inhabits them. In contrast, diversity and cross-cultural research theorizes workplaces as static containers for different groups of people. Such a theory of work and organizations does not account for the ways in which narratives of belonging, nationhood, and race/ethnicity may materialize in workplace encounters and consequently impact how people understand themselves and others.

The final element that warrants attention is material practices—such practices involve the material ways in which people may engage in transnational communities as it relates to their belief systems, social activities, and political engagement. The material focuses on those aspects of one's life that are defined, constrained, and reassembled by the various social, cultural, and political structures in which people are embedded. For example, the ways in which a person votes for people and/or on issues in their communities and in national elections that take place in other countries. While there is some focus on these kinds of behaviors and material practices by way of literature on diaspora communities (Brah, 2005; Hall, 2014) including those focusing on voting practices (Waterbury, 2010), the focus on transnational subjectivities in relation to hybrids opens up discussion around the relationship of the material to the formation of subjects. In this sense, voting (or any other material practice) defines subjectivities and subjectivities define which material practices are deemed important to enact. By contrast, diaspora as a concept does not address the new forms through which being and belonging take shape in different contexts as the concept of diaspora makes sense only in relation to a pre-defined or pre-determined homeland or part of a nation-state. Hybridity requires particular kinds of material practices (veiling/unveiling as one example), including those in workplaces and organizational settings, to take form and, in doing so, speaks to novel transnational forms of subjects.

What difference for MOS?

In sum, the concept of hybridity is a novel subject that stands to provide new insights about the ways in which subjectivities emerge. Specifically, hybrid subjectivities take shape through epistemic, social, and material dimensions and agentic, reflexive practices across transnational scales. By theorizing subjects in such a manner, we open up opportunities for rethinking the very people we study under the umbrella of diversity and difference research in the context of MOS. In the US business school context, diversity and cross-cultural experiences are now required parts of AACSB (Association to Advance Collegiate Schools of Business) accreditation. Specifically, 'inclusion and diversity' are required values associated with the accreditation process while diversity is seen as a corporate social responsibility dimension highly relevant for developing global leaders and managers (AACSB, 2018). In this sense, there is growing pressure and recognition to address diversity as an important part of organizational life such that educating future leaders and managers now requires including diversity topics.

Yet in examining the ways diversity has been theorized and researched, there is still much room for improvement as it relates to understanding the complexity of subjects at work and how organizations themselves are sites and places for encounters. Namely, there needs to be much more attention to encounters between/among people in a transnational manner. By doing so, MOS scholars can begin to theorize and understand how the 'mixings' of ideas, cultures, and notions of race/ethnicity take shape in workplaces. As a result, the traditional ways in which tensions and conflict are thought to arise may not necessarily be due to differences in cultural values and identities but may be due to challenges to unvoiced assumptions around nationhood and belonging. The majority of research in diversity and difference yields insights, albeit in a limited fashion, about the ways people understand themselves, and examines differences in experiences and the values of such differences for contributions at work: much more is necessary to understand the ways transnational subjectivities interrupt static and bounded notions of self. By acknowledging hybridity as an emergent form of subjectivity in the context of work, MOS scholars can yield insights about the form and function of organizations not (only) as sites of productive economic activity but also as sites of epistemic, social, and material practices.

Hybridity challenges the very notions of national, cultural, and racial/ethnic boundaries as represented by the concept of identity. In doing so, it begets questions and concerns around the value of research that purports to replicate existing ways of differentiating people. Hybridity is not simply a better analytic tool but is also an ethical consideration and engagement with the very theoretical tools in the MOS field. How might the ways in which we assign value to difference be reconsidered if we acknowledge assumptions about race/ethnicity, nationhood and belonging embedded in our theories and research endeavors? Hybridity opens up epistemological opportunities for not only producing a different kind of research subject as it relates to theorizing and understanding differences but also bringing to bear an ethical consideration. If the research we produce is used to 'educate' the next generation of business leaders and global managers, how are dominant notions of difference and value being perpetuated through the curriculum, research, and practices we adopt?

In answering this question, scholarship attending to difference must acknowledge that the very assumptions of the field are embedded in ideas about transgressions, ethics, and equity. The leading concerns around team outcomes and organizational performance (and others) as they relate to diversity and culture are essentially questions and concerns about people entering spaces (such as workplaces and other organizations) that have yet to acknowledge their unspoken rules, norms, and assumptions. As Wingfield and Alston (2014) note, organizations that are predominantly White engage in organizational practices and dole out tasks that create and maintain racial hierarchies. Similarly, Liu (2016b) contends that Whiteness is an organizing principle in many organizations, resulting in many organizations being stratified by race (Wooten and Couloute, 2017). The concern then is whether and how diversity and cross-cultural concepts unwittingly replicate racial and other inequalities in organizations when they do not challenge toxic Whiteness, a point that is taken up further in Chapter 7.

Hybridity then is not only a concern about a new subjectivity but also an epistemic call toward a new ethics of research into differences. It calls into question existing categories of difference and how those categories are called on to potentially continue stratifying, segregating, and limiting the options and experiences available for transnational selves which defy organizational (and hence societal) expectations around belonging and nationhood. In calling into question the way race, culture, and other categories for identifying individuals are used in diversity and cross-cultural research, hybridity as an analytic lens suspends clearly defined binaries, categories and notions of self. Ultimately, hybridity opens up opportunities for studying new subjectivities at work by way of epistemic, social, and material considerations in a transnational mode. In doing so, it calls on scholars to acknowledge guiding assumptions around the historic context of encounters, the consequences of continuing to use identity categories and the ethical considerations associated with the very foundation of seeking out 'differences'.

5

Cosmopolitans

As the final chapter expanded on the new agentic, reflexive subjectivities arising from transnational migration, the focus herein is on cosmopolitanism and cosmopolitans. The first section of the chapter underscores the main tenets of cosmopolitanism and cosmopolitans and thereby offers insights into the various ways this notion has been theorized. This sets the stage for empirical examples of cosmopolitanism in research that takes shape at the intersections of global business, work, and difference. These examples challenge the notion of cosmopolitanism as referencing people who have a global mindset and are 'citizens of everywhere and nowhere' (Levy et al., 2007)—approaches which dominate cross-cultural management and examinations of difference in a global context. In contrast to this idea of cosmopolitanism, a transnational migration studies offers a multiscalar perspective that uncovers the granularity and performative aspects of this concept inclusive of its ethical dimensions. The third section focuses on the ways 'global nomad' as an example of cosmopolitanism challenges financialized notions of diversity in the context of organizations and neoliberalism. The focus herein is on the ways ethics and labor intersect as people construct ways of being and belonging to the world through their agentic economic activities. In concluding this chapter, the final consideration is around the link of cosmopolitanism to an ethics of difference that embodies the epistemic, social, and material aspects of transnational being and belonging. By addressing these concerns in the context of MOS research, the goal is to offer new directions in relation to the quest for theorizing and accounting for various forms of difference in relation to people and work.

Conceptualizing cosmopolitanism and cosmopolitans: agency, tastes and ethics

In the context of globalization, the movement of workers across national borders has received much attention in the international management literature, including research that aims to understand the ways 'brain circulation' contributes to the upskilling of organizations and regions (Tung, 2008b). Despite its origin in Saxenian's (2005) seminal work on transnational ties, immigrants and upskilling, 'brain circulation' of skilled workers and immigrants in the context of international and cross-cultural management has focused almost explicitly on their 'value' for organizations, such as in being cultural intermediaries for Western multinational corporations and Chinese locals (Hartmann et al., 2010), and on understanding the effectiveness of their international careers across cultures (Tams and Arthur, 2007) including ways to differentiate between self and assigned expatriates (Biemann and Andresen, 2010). The adoption of only certain elements from the broader concept of 'brain circulation' leaves unattended the various structural, political, and socio-cultural dimensions that give rise to the ability of certain people to circulate. By focusing only on the cognitive cultural elements of the concept, the international and cross-cultural management field attends to difference in the same static way—by focusing on the psychological dimensions rather than the history, context, and practices associated with the movement of such individuals, the field cannot attend fully examine the consequences of ontological mobility.

The concept of 'brain circulation' when it makes its way to the MOS field ends up being reproduced as 'global mindset' (Story and Barbuto Jr, 2011), defined as the development of cultural intelligence and a global business outlook derived from travel and experiences of different cultures. This mindset approach replicates many of the problematic issues discussed in Chapter 1 around theorizing culture as cognition rather than as a historic, agentic, and reflexive practice. By focusing on mindset, scholarship aims to outline those elements that are deemed important for managing people and organizations in a global context. In other words, the global mindset is seen as a tool or mechanism that can allow for effective control and oversight of people in culturally different contexts across organizations. Rather than understand or value the ways in which people may develop a sense of themselves in a world on-the-move, the approach in MOS is to consider how such a mindset can be replicated for the benefit of the organization.

Yet the 'global mindset' and similar approaches that equate culture with psychological schemas, values, and norms do not attend to the complexity of transnational subjectivities that act with agency and in a reflexive fashion. Moreover, they do not consider or examine the (unspoken) ethics of extracting labor from cultural Others. To examine these issues and to speak to the third and final contribution related to subjectivity arising from transnational migration studies, here I expand on the concept of cosmopolitanism by drawing its relevant points for theorizing people on-the-move. My focus in this third subjectivity arising from transnational migration studies frameworks is to focus on issues of agency, taste, and ethics.

In simple terms, cosmopolitanism is a way of relating to the world and a particular set of epistemic, social, and material practices. Mendieta (2009: 342) states:

> cosmopolitanism is both an epistemic and moral relationship to the historical world of humans, for it seeks to know and recognize humanity in everything that humans have accomplished. Cosmopolitanism, therefore, even if in an attenuated form, also entails a 'cosmopolitan' project in which some sort of legal political institutional framework would allow for the cohabitation and mutual thriving of all that is singular, and thus different, and differentiating in humanity.

Cosmopolitanism can be conceptualized as an orientation toward locally grounded experiences while at the same time recrafting one's tastes, ideas, and practices in relation to global reference points, such as popular culture and media. This reflexive approach challenges cosmopolitanism's epistemic origins as the *habitus* of cultural and social elites (Hannerz, 2004) and the transnational capitalist class (Sklair, 2001) and toward the inclusion of marginal people and positions including those based on social class (see Werbner, 2006). In other words, cosmopolitanism is a 'grounded social category' than necessarily an abstract or ideal notion of personhood under conditions of globalization and mobility (Skrbis et al., 2004). It challenges notions of disembodied 'global' people who are traversing the globe given that it inscribes an ethical dimension into mobility. Transnational modes force (re)consideration around the social, economic, and political conditions that make movement possible or, in some cases, impossible.

At the same time, this agentic, reflexive mode of theorizing cosmopolitans stands in contrast to other ways that have been used to theorize its boundaries and dimensions. Vertovec and Cohen (2003: 9–14) note that there are six perspectives when theorizing cosmopolitanism, including as a socio-cultural condition, a philosophy/worldview, a political project related to transnational institutions, a political project related to multiple subjects, a disposition, or a practice. These various conceptualizations lend themselves to debate and discussion but for the purposes of this book, I rely more on Mendieta's (2009) approach to open up space for the various different ways in which cosmopolitanism can be manifest particularly in relation to work and organizations. Specifically, this conceptualization allows consideration of the intersections of work and mobility: in the context of globally dispersed gendered and racialized production networks (Barrientos et al., 2011), who moves under what conditions and for what ends needs to be primary for analyses of self, difference, and work.

On this point, Benhabib (2008) suggests that cosmopolitanism must attend to the ethos that inscribes particular people to a nation but, at the same time, strips away the rights of others. Appiah suggests that cosmopolitanism underscores the fact that people have obligations beyond their family, friends, and those with whom they share citizenship and, that in studying human lives, we understand the 'practices and beliefs that lend [lives] significance' (Appiah, 2010: xv). In examples of empirical work that speak to these conceptual observations, Katz-Gerro (2017) finds that individuals consume 'non-national' culture within Europe based on availability and opportunity. In other words, there is both agency and reflexivity in how people may choose to engage with cultural aesthetics that are associated with a different people or nation-state. In her study of Romanians in London, Moroşanu (2018) suggests that people need to negotiate ethnic differences and boundaries in the context of cosmopolitan sociability rather than attempt to reconcile them. As such, there is no given or guidelines around how to 'be cosmopolitan' but rather, depending on the context, different transnational modes in the domain of the epistemic, social, and material are called on to create a sense of self.

Beyond agency, such practices take shape across social classes such that the critique of cosmopolitanism being the domain of the elite is challenged. Within this context, several examples of cosmopolitanism serve as a counter point to the notions of personhood present in international management where people 'collect' and deploy cultural experiences as needed without consideration of the ethical and reflexive dimensions of such practices. Moreover, cosmopolitanism by way of these examples also challenges the control and power imperative in diversity and cross-cultural management research—how to manage those individuals who are 'different' while at the same time extracting their labor in appropriate ways without attending to the ethics or epistemologies of difference. The examples herein speak to the very notions of cosmopolitanism but do so in the context of work and organizations such that they are relevant for critiquing extant MOS work on difference in relation to the points around ethics and reflexivity. They also provide counterpoints to the narrow idea of 'global mindset' and culture as conceptual tools for theorizing the complex subjectivities of transnational selves.

On the performative: being and belonging to the world in a cosmopolitan fashion

The first example speaks to issues at the intersections of ethics, agency and reflexivity in a transnational mode as Colic-Peisker (2010) focuses on diverse transnational knowledge workers in Australia and Indonesia. She examines serially mobile individuals whose careers span working in at least three different nations and follows the ways they craft a sense of cosmopolitanism anchored in affinities and attachments with their professions, specific locales, social networks, and local communities. Her research underscores that the notion of belonging is an inextricable part of such workers who are reflect some autonomy in their ability to move between jobs and nations given they are not employees of one organization that may require them to move globally. Given that visas are an important and relevant part of any conversation on movement, Colic-Peisker (2010: 477) finds that avoiding speaking about nation-states is impossible given they are 'the final arbiters of transnational mobility'. Respondents relied on a particular national identity depending on whether they thought it was useful for a specific context or relationship. Thus, belonging to a particular nation-state was only relevant in as much as it was about prestige, or allowed access to or information about something/someone that would have otherwise been not available. In some cases, choosing not to reveal one's national identity was an agentic response to previous experiences of discrimination in being paid less for the same work due their 'country of origin'. In all, respondents chose to craft a sense of self that amalgamated different experiences, bringing together a subjectivity that was both reflexive but also strategically appropriate for the specific work and context.

In this example, cosmopolitanism is a way to speak about selves *beyond the nation* by relying on transnational social fields, but it also an engagement with ethics: the nation-state is a slippery identity category deployed by the individual to 'make sense' in relation to those they meet. Nationality is a conventional way to present oneself rather than a sense of identity (Colic-Peisker, 2010: 477). Consequently, the agentic unbounding of identity from nation and reconstruction of a reflexive subjectivity simultaneously reconfigures the ethos of nation: nations do not claim individuals, but individuals claim nations in reflexive ways. Through the agentic disavowal and remaking of the terms of belonging that nations require of citizens, subjectivity emerges through an ethical engagement and a transnational practice. In this example, such unbounding becomes necessary in moments when potential discrimination or work tension is deemed imminent. In these instances, the individuals make a choice about which repertoire of experiences, practices, and ideas to engage in order to present themselves in a fashion that is reflexive but also self-preserving. The self created and presented in such an encounter relies on a particular narrative of nationhood to create a sense of belonging, which may be challenged by another party. During the myriad encounters that take shape during one's professional work, narratives of nationhood alongside ethico-epistemic practices of self-naming (or silencing) one's nation-state intersect to create a cosmopolitan sense of self.

Consequently, cosmopolitanism speaks to those people and moments in which transnational modes of being and belonging arise from very specific epistemic, social, and material practices. With each movement to a new work context, a reassessment and remaking of selves takes shape through the ways in which individuals identify themselves in terms of ethnicity, citizenship, and community. Each movement requires a renegotiation of self based on encounters with new people, relationships, and organizational practices that are taking shape while at the same time relying on older or rehearsed repertoires of subjectivity. In such instances, cosmopolitanism allows examination of the presentation of self as both an ethical and an epistemic practice. The social practices associated with such an ethico-epistemic move are also relevant in that they speak to the ways in which customs, norms and practices from one context are then seeded in another context through the movement of people. People become carriers and consumers of ideas, which then leads to new and emergent social practices in their place of work. Finally, the material dimension speaks to those ways of being a 'knowledge worker' in different contexts and may require the uptake and deployment of particular work habits and norms. These may be emergent based on context but may also be derived from previous experience working in communities such that work habits and norms end up traveling as practices to new workplaces. The power of cosmopolitanism as a conceptual lens is to outline how such travel and translations take shape by acknowledging the agentic, reflexive, and ethical dimensions embedded in the work.

In all, the ways of understanding mobile workers available from a transnational migration studies framework broadly and cosmopolitanism specifically stands in stark contrast to a similarly focused international management study on knowledge nomads or knowledge workers who move frequently between different jobs, organizations, and homes. To demonstrate this difference, here I juxtapose the previous study with another one on globally mobile knowledge workers. In doing so, the goal is to demonstrate key differences between the contributions of cosmopolitanism and cosmopolitans as a subjectivity to the very ideas and concepts deployed in MOS to study the 'same' subject: global knowledge workers. As expanded on through the example, the start and end of the conversation on the same topic is vastly different from a cosmopolitanism lens versus the cognitive cultural and control framework available in the MOS literature.

In their work, Pittinsky and Shih (2004) focus on best ways to manage mobile knowledge workers given that their mobile nature may make them seem less committed to the organization. Relying on insights from positive organizational scholarship (POS), the authors aim to demonstrate that previous work, which cast such mobile workers in a negative light, may be shortsighted and incomplete. Instead, they suggest such employees can still have organizational commitment if they are managed appropriately and derive a set of ideas from POS to change negative psychological frames about mobile workers. In other words, they showcase that deep commitment to work defines mobile employees and such employees stand to make positive contributions to the overall wellbeing of the organization. They also hope that their research can impact workforce development conversations around the support and development of such employees. In all, the scholars work toward highlighting the positive benefits of such workers despite negative connotations and perceptions associated with mobile workers including low morale, limited motivation, and high turnover rates.

Consequently, even when mobility is acknowledged in MOS, it is done so with a sense of loss: what might the organization lose if such workers are employed and how best to mitigate that potential loss? The primacy of employee productivity corrupts any sense of ethics as a sense of belonging to/in the world and instead, only offers a neoliberal version of it that prioritizes a sense of belonging or commitment to the organization as the means to extract labor. Any other sense of belonging people might have is seen as competing with their allegiance to the organization and, instead, the employee is only valuable to the organization if s/he is seen as 'committed'. These concerns lead to researchers to outline ways in which such employees might need to be incentivized or managed in order to remain committed to the organization. The focus then is on employee retention to maximize their utility for the organization given the employee's deep commitment to work. The ability to do work, in this case, is the primary contributor to the mobile employee's value in the organization. Mobility and attendant changes in self, ideas, and practices accompanying it are irrelevant as long as they do not interfere with such the ability of that person to become a committed employee. By narrating mobility in terms of employer–employee relations and expectations, MOS research fails to make clear the structural, ethical, and political dimensions of why employees may want to leave workplaces and organizations that treat them only as resources. Difference only matters in as much as organizations can figure out how to draw out commitment and labor from mobile workers in the most appropriate ways.

Ahmed (2016) calls such regulatory behaviors 'diversity work', that set of behaviors, norms, and actions that must be adopted for individuals to 'fit' into existing structures of work, organizations, and society. In the context of organizations, the assumption is that some level of change or preparing is necessary when the 'Other' starts to occupy those spaces and sites that have been associated with dominant groups. Transgressions in this space, people occupying positions historically not associated with them, or behaving in ways that are deemed 'inappropriate' are cause for work including the 'management' of differences and different people. Mobile workers then require diversity work on the part of organizations inclusive of training, new HRM practices to engage them fully or workforce development interventions. Yet there little is done to understand why diversity work is assumed to be necessary in the first place, a conversation that would necessitate addressing notions of 'fit' on cultural or other terms as well as discussions on what constitutes commitment and productivity in organizations. To address these concerns and their underlying epistemologies, it is necessary to understand the ethics of theorizing and studying differences—a consideration in the final chapter of this book.

Two additional examples that focus on everyday practices illustrate the lived experiences of the broader philosophical issues related to nation, ethics, and cosmopolitan subjectivity. Datta (2009: 353) focuses on how East European construction workers in London are 'shaped by their transnational histories, nationalistic sentiments, and access to social and cultural capital in specific localised contexts' to provide a sense of how mobile working class laborers exemplify cosmopolitanism in their daily lives through consumption of cultural products, food, and media. In their study, Nowicka and Kaweh (2009) examine the everyday practices of UN professionals who move every two years to a new location and engage in new cultural encounters. The uprooting and re-rooting of these individuals take shape through a repertoire of practices that they adopt and bring with them. At the same time, there are contradictions that emerge whereby in the encounters there are 'struggles for meaningful engagement with the locals' (Nowicka and Kaweh, 2009: 88). The scholars focus on how individuals modulate their encounters with others through their foreign language skills, social networks, schooling, housing and shopping opportunities, as well as the ways they spend their spare time (2009: 90).

In both examples, the research brings to light how each new context and location offers new opportunities for the performative: deploying a particular set of everyday practices and repertoires, a translating of self, ideas, and practices on the go. These new productions of subjectivity take place in relation to social class and tastes as well as an ethics of engagement with the rest of the world: an orientation to self and others in the world that arrives not out of culture-writ mental programming but through agentic and reflexive assembling of transnational lives. To underscore another dimension of such subjectivities, I focus next on global nomads as an exemplar of contemporary cosmopolitanism at the intersections of agentic economic activity, ethical mobility, and neoliberalism.

Global nomads

As a specific form of cosmopolitanism, global nomads represent those individuals who circulate in the global economy. These individuals do not circulate as 'expatriates' or as 'mobile professionals' but through their nomadic economic endeavors which are contingent and context specific. Global nomads, by choice and opportunity, are engaged in the reconstitution of economic value through exchange relations that take shape as they travel globally on their own terms. More specifically, they can be conceptualized as those individuals who:

> embody a specific type of agency informed by cultural motivations that defy economic rationale. Many of them have abandoned urban hubs where they enjoyed a favorable material status (income, stability, prestige), and migrated to semi-peripheral locations with a pleasant climate, in order to dedicate themselves to the shaping of an alternative lifestyle … they retain the cultural capital that would allow them to revert to previous life schemes if necessary … they define new economic goals when entering alternative niches of art, wellness, therapy and entertainment, catering to tourists and wealthy residents as well as to other neo-nomads (D'Andrea, 2006: 98).

This subjectivity challenges economic discussions of diversity and the ways in which we conceptualize people who travel or are mobile in relation to work. At the same time, being a global nomad is a social and economic privilege, and ultimately a subjectivity undertaken through choice (Vertovec, 2001) in contrast to similarly mobile people—refugees—who are forced to move and remake their lives due to social and political unrest, war, or environmental catastrophe, among other reasons. Thus, here I focus on those people who can make a choice in how and why they move including the ways they remake notions of economic value particularly in the context of work. The chapter on inequality (Chapter 7) attends much more closely to these concerns around (im)mobility and forced mobility, including its consequences for the production, replication, and maintenance of various organizational inequities. The main concern herein is the fact that such globally mobile individuals in the context of the work cannot be sufficiently understood through the existing conceptual conventions of diversity and cross-cultural research. Moreover, the ways in which such mobility is maintained through various infrastructures including organizational contexts is both an important consideration and a valuable contribution to research in/around difference. How do organizational contexts and work settings provide various opportunities and spaces for mobility? Moreover, how do workplaces require particular economic exchange activities that may result in potentially exacerbating extant inequalities?

To this end, organizations become more than contexts for extracting labor and exchange relations between and among culturally different others: they are sites of the production of subjectivities and, thus, theorizing them only as arenas for the extraction of labor does not suffice. In other words, any attempt to reconsider the ways difference and diversity work takes shape must also attend to the organizational norms and values that are being espoused in the search for difference. The ways in which organizations act as sites of encounter between culturally different people are notable. In such encounters, opportunities arise for rethinking underlying cultural and racial hierarchies. These hierarchies arise when particular labor and organizational roles are allocated and/or assigned to cultural Others with an understanding that they are not as prestigious, such as the experiences of Black healthcare workers (Wingfield, 2019). Yet what happens when the very subjects of such research do not fit neatly into boxes given transnational modes of being and belonging, and cosmopolitan (and nomadic) subjectivities? Do the ways we think about and examine difference in relation to organizational work (as economic activity) also need to change?

To expand on this point, it is important to recognize that a large segment of diversity research examines the performance-related aspects of difference in workplaces and organizational settings broadly defined.

In this vein, there are several streams of research including those focused on the impact of diversity on individual organizational attachment (Tsui et al., 1992), leadership (Eagly and Chin, 2010), mentoring relationships (Ensher and Murphy, 1997; Conboy and Kelly, 2016), and firm financial performance based on board diversity (Campbell and Mínguez-Vera, 2008; Rose, 2007), top-management team diversity (Kilduff et al., 2000), and ethnic diversity (Andrevski et al., 2014). A significant portion of diversity research has also focused on its impact on group and team processes and outcomes (McLeod et al., 1996; Milliken and Martins, 1996; Chatman and Flynn, 2001; Ely and Thomas, 2001; Mannix and Neale, 2005; Horwitz and Horwitz, 2007; Chatman, 2010; Pieterse et al., 2013; Srikanth et al., 2016) in organizational contexts. In all, there is a concern over the performance dimensions of diversity and difference, and a significant concern over implementing the 'right' management and HR practices that will lead to productivity gains and competitive advantage for the organization. These are all concerns that dominate the MOS field and drive the ways in which difference is used, at times, to advocate for particular organizational changes or programs.

While on the surface such calls may be seen as neutral or even beneficial to women and minorities, their assumptions related to why such change might be necessary are left unvoiced—this is where the intervention of transnational analysis modes is necessary: it opens up the possibilities for how experiences within organizations may differ not based on categories of race and gender but instead based on the ways in which people actively engage in epistemic, social and material transnational practices. These ways of being and belonging are not acknowledged when the guiding norms in the MOS field around difference are based on categories of identity that are specific to US history, context, and businesses. Moreover, many research approaches share an underlying assumption about the 'return on diversity' or, as is more commonly known, they are representative of the 'business case' for diversity research (Cox and Blake, 1991; Robinson and Dechant, 1997; Herring, 2009). Thus, MOS research that claims to be looking at differences does so at the intersections of neoliberalism and value creation such that accounting for the value of 'difference' has led to more efficient ways to extract labor from those deemed different. As a consequence, the theorizing and accounting for difference is not a neutral engagement but entangled with the axioms of financialization and neoliberalism creeping into our daily lives and the social world more broadly.

Yet the notion of global nomads not only offers a new form of agentic, reflexive subjectivity, but it also disrupts the financialization of diversity and its underlying economic rationale. People become nomads with the aim of undertaking new economic value creation activities that do not play by the rules of the neoliberalism game as exemplified in organizational efforts to gain economic returns on diversity or 'managing difference'. Global nomads as a framework for attending to subjectivity speaks to broader socio-political and economic trends whereby individuals attempt to work within the cracks and peripheries of neoliberalism (Gibson-Graham, 1997; Kingfisher and Maskovsky, 2008) in crafting their own transnational lives and, while related, this approach is not the same as the equally important and growing social justice perspective on diversity (Tomlinson and Schwabenland, 2010; Thompson, 2016) in contrast to the business case for diversity. That is, such individuals assemble nomadic lives not necessarily for social justice but to escape the confines of economic productivity discourses in organizational contexts. Global nomads emerge through the political, ethical, and affective economies of dispossession (Butler and Athanasiou, 2013) and their breaking away from the extractive labor arrangements of formal organizations represents an opening up of the political and social imaginary. What new possibilities for reorganizing economies and societies might there be if we 'read organizations critically' through the lens of nomadism and dispossession?

In this sense, 'global nomad' as a concept speaks to those possibilities around subjectivity arising at the intersections of economic activity, ethics, and value creation. This iteration of cosmopolitanism focuses explicitly on the value creation and labor-extraction motive associated with workplaces under conditions of neoliberalism. Yet global nomad offers a glimpse into the possibility that individuals can craft their own sense of self derived from transnational economic activities that cut across the epistemic, social, and material domains. The ethico-epistemic practice is the denial of a self that is only accounted for and recognized in financialized terms through the language of diversity and difference—expatriate, global knowledge worker, and other appellations are fraught with assumptions around their value for organizations. Rather, nomad eschews these categories in favor of a fluid but transnationally scaled self that emerges from work undertaken under conditions determined by the individual. Second, the social practices associated with this subjectivity are in the domain of lifestyle—that is, global nomad is a lifestyle and an economic activity. As such, it is not a phase but a choice. Finally, the material elements of global nomad speak to those very practices of creating and sustaining a life on-the-move replete with challenges around visas, legality of work, political engagement, and healthcare, among other issues. In effect, without the boundaries of the organization around them, global nomads craft their own border and boundaries around their lives and work—a creative and ethical activity that is relevant for rethinking what organizations look like in the context of transnational migration.

The ethics of theorizing difference

In all, the foundations of the international management field broadly and cross-cultural management field specifically are based on concerns of what happens when culturally different people: 1) encounter each other in work contexts; 2) attempt to work together; and 3) create value for the organization including its globally dispersed units. Yet the assumptions guiding why culturally different individuals may be 'problematic' are not addressed in much of the literature. There is little concern over why 'extracting' value from them might raise ethical concerns in the context of neoliberalism. While there have been some critical discussions and interjections as outlined in Chapter 1, much of the field remains engaged in conversations that adopt static notions of culture derived from Western psychological constructs. Moreover, the ways in which the international business processes and practices as they relate to extracting value from culturally different individuals are not examined critically particularly in the context of race/ethnicity, belonging, and nationhood. Rather, the concern is around mitigating any tensions, conflict, or challenges that might arise in such workplaces while at the same extracting maximum value from such workers. As a point of contrast, cosmopolitans as an exemplar of agentic, reflexive subjectivities necessitate consideration of the ethical dimensions of mobility and our theories about difference.

In thinking further about this point, the ways in which difference becomes theorized, researched, valued, and reproduced raises questions related to the epistemological foundations of the diversity and cross-cultural management field. How we produce knowledge about difference is a fundamentally core question about the values and ethics we espouse as scholars interested in uncovering the value of diversity and culture. Yet in adopting frameworks that embody and reflect unspoken assumptions about economic value, belonging, and nationhood, are we truly producing 'value free scientific knowledge'? Rather, we are producing knowledge that locates the value of difference in its ability to extract a different kind of labor from individuals: difference is the new currency of globalized neoliberalism. Similar to Young's observations related to the ways culture was a genre of analysis based on racial hierarchies separating out 'primitive' from 'civilized' nations (Young, 1995/2005), the focus on difference in the MOS literature requires an understanding of its origins and goals. In other words, what is accomplished by theorizing difference through the axioms of race/ethnicity, culture, and nationhood?

Cosmopolitanism, and cosmopolitan as a new subjectivity, calls on researchers to understand the intersections of nationhood, agency, tastes, and ethics—but more so for a conversation on the ways in which ideas about race/ethnicity and belonging are developed and deployed in research settings. As a subjectivity, cosmopolitans speak to those ways of being and belonging to the social world which arise from habits, tastes, and experiences that evolve and are negotiated in the context of particular nation-states. Rather than attributing tastes to a particular class or ethnicity, the expanded examples presented in this chapter allow consideration for the negotiated nature of such subjectivities and their engagement with boundary creation. How boundaries between different race/ethnic groups or between one's self and 'Others' are created is a powerful mechanism for understanding why particular tensions might be taking shape in workplaces and organizational contexts.

In thinking about these issues, and all three subjectivities that have been presented in these chapters so far (transmigrants, hybrids and cosmopolitans), there is shared concern around agency and reflexivity. Yet each of them speaks to a specific and different aspect of transnational subjectivity. Transmigrants speaks to those ways in which transnational selves are created through the use of transnational social fields across scales and, in the context of MOS, these ways of being and belonging expand on the ways difference is theorized and researched. The second subjectivity, hybrids, builds on the agentic and reflexive dimensions of transnational selves but adds a layer of complexity by underscoring the emergent and hybrid (and even ambiguous) ways people create a sense of being and belonging. Hybridity opens up opportunities to understand how, across transnational scales, creative and novel epistemic, social, and material practices give way to new selves. These selves cannot be represented by static identity or cognitive cultural categories no matter their relational or additive approaches (such as bi-culturals or multiculturals). Finally, cosmopolitanism and cosmopolitans speak to those agentic and reflexive elements of subjectivity but with a keen focus on agency and the ethics of being and belonging. The epistemic, social, and material dimensions of creating a sense across new contexts is done through an intentional ethical engagement and consideration. In work contexts, this allows remaking the ways in which value is allocated to individuals who are deemed 'different' such that new conceptualizations around belonging emerge on terms created by mobile individuals.

Moving MOS forward

Taken together, these subjectivities provide new depth and insights around how we theorize the subject of work as it relates to differences and understanding difference. Yet much more is necessary than theorizing different subjectivities. In this regards, the next three chapters provide new directions for research in MOS notably by focusing on the topic of inequality, reconceptualizing multiculturalism and, finally, by offering methodologies which can attend to mobile subjects. In all, the next three chapters provide new directions for the broad field of MOS in changing the language around how we theorize people and work in a mobile world.

Chapter 6 focuses on multiculturalism as an important and growing area which needs attention in MOS—the chapter outlines how extant work in MOS does not and cannot attend to multiculturalism as the new form of society. As such, the ways in which difference are theorized do not attend to the large-scale changes taking shape across societies globally as transnational migration (re)makes existing categories of race/ethnicity and pushes the boundaries on who or what constitutes nationhood. Through these changes, new conversations around multiculturalism and belonging arise and are relevant for how we theorize how work is done and who does what kinds of work in our societies and economies.

Chapter 7 focuses explicitly on inequality as a necessary and important consideration into any examination of subjectivities in a globalized, neoliberal world economy. The ways in which transnational migration impacts lives is beyond new forms of subjectivity and the chapter on inequality provides the context for understanding these issues. It also addresses the shortcomings of MOS research in not attending sufficiently to issues of inequality, particularly in relation to the foundations of searching for 'difference' and in relation to the ways in which organizations extract labor from cultural Others.

Chapter 8 offers methodologies that can attend to mobile subjects through examples and expanded discussion around why mobility must change the research approaches generally deployed in the diversity and cross-cultural management fields. The chapter focuses on alternative ways that researchers can attend to mobility inclusive of mobile subjects not only as people but as a particular set of ideas or practices. By contrasting mobile methodologies with existing approaches, the chapter offers new directions for scholars who are interested in attending to and researching mobility.

PART III

Transnational Approaches: New Directions and Challenges for the Field

6

Diversity Research After Mobility: Multiculturalism

> In today's global politics of identity and difference, the migration condition is symptomatically central for [Stuart] Hall, for it speaks through a 'double syntax' in which difference may be driven toward the all-or-nothing danger of ethnic absolutism—or it may … enable us to learn something from diasporic survival about how to live with others and otherness.
>
> Kobena Mercer, introduction to Stuart Hall (1994/2017), *The Fateful Triangle: Race, Ethnicity and Nation*, pp 10–11

Contextualizing migration

Migration has been one of the most pronounced ways through which societies have transformed over the course of history. According to the United Nations (UN) migration report for 2017, there were about 258 million migrants globally, up from 220 million in 2010 and 173 million in 2000 (see Table 1). While much of the extant theories and theorizing about migration has taken shape in Europe and North America in regard to 'incoming' migrants, the reality is that Asia to Asia migration is the biggest flow of people, and 106 million of the 258 million global migrants were born in Asia. Between 2000 and 2017, Asia gained about 30 million migrants followed by Europe at 22 million and North America at 17 million.

At the same, more than 50% of all international migrants live in ten countries and areas, with the largest number residing in the United States (50 million or about 19% of the world's migratory population). This was followed by Saudi Arabia, Germany and the Russian Federation with each

Table 1: 2017 International migrant stock by major area of origin and destination

	Origin							
	Africa	Asia	Europe	Latin America and the Caribbean	Northern America	Oceania	Unknown	**World**
Africa	19,359,848	1,225,453	966,505	30,925	65,946	21,135	2,980,411	**24,650,223**
Asia	4,430,864	63,277,439	7,118,198	444,725	504,368	94,532	3,716,583	**79,586,709**
Europe	9,322,904	20,463,256	41,030,520	4,607,113	1,030,770	350,588	1,090,066	**77,895,217**
Latin America and the Caribbean	55,825	349,538	1,342,089	6,094,226	1,361,188	7,049	298,274	**9,508,189**
Northern America	2,571,436	17,201,010	7,630,396	26,382,585	1,217,801	283,267	2,377,659	**57,664,154**
Oceania	525,551	3,167,398	3,103,192	160,424	233,215	1,123,905	97,248	**8,410,933**
Grand total	**36,266,428**	**105,684,094**	**61,190,900**	**37,719,998**	**4,413,288**	**1,880,476**	**10,560,241**	**257,715,425**

Source: December 2017 – Copyright © 2017 by United Nations. All rights reserved.
Suggested citation: United Nations, Department of Economic and Social Affairs, Population Division (2017).
Trends in International Migrant Stock: The 2017 Revision (United Nations database, POP/DB/MIG/Stock/Rev.2017).

of them hosting around 12 million migrants each. In the US, immigrants represent about 15.3% of the entire population, in Saudi Arabia, 37% of the population, in Germany, 14.8% of the population and in the Russian Federation, they represent 8.1% (Migration Policy Institute, 2017). Perhaps most urgently, the number of refugees and asylum seekers due to forced displacement has continued to rise with the developing world hosting around 83% of the world's refugees and asylum seekers. In this context, Turkey had the largest refugee population globally, hosting about 3.1 million of such migrants due to growing humanitarian crisis and war in neighboring countries, most urgently in Syria. In all, these numbers indicate that there are several trends that are relevant for how we theorize transnational aspects of migration.

First, there are clear ways in which certain nation-states are connected to others in the context of migratory flows. For example, migrants from Mexico to the US represent the largest population from a single country living in a single country of destination. In 2017, there were around 13 million Mexicans who migrated to the US. Similarly, other 'bilateral corridors' or migratory movements between pairs of countries (UN, 2017: 14) can be seen for India to the United Arab Emirates (3.3 million), China to the US (2.4 million) as well as China to Hong Kong (2.3 million), and Bangladesh to India (3.1 million). Interestingly, there are also examples of mutual and equal migratory flows in terms of population. Migratory flows from Russian Federation to Ukraine and Ukraine to Russian Federation each account for 3.3 million migrants respectively. Similarly, Kazakhstan to Russian Federation is around 2.6 million while Russian Federation to Kazakhstan is 2.4 million (UN, 2017).

Second, in order to understand the ways in which societies are changing in contemporary times due to migration, it is imperative to become familiar with the ways in which movement is taking shape. In 2017, the 20 largest countries/areas of origin accounted for about half of all international migrants with about 34% of all international migrants originating in ten countries. The UN (2017: 12) notes, 'India is now the country with the largest number of people living outside the country's borders ("diaspora"), followed by Mexico, the Russian Federation and China'. The top ten migrant sending countries include India, Mexico, Russian Federation, China, Bangladesh, Syrian Arab Republic, Pakistan, Ukraine, Philippines and the UK (UN, 2017: 13). As a result, there are certain countries whose entire economies are either highly dependent or almost exclusively dependent on immigrant workers and labor. While there are different ways in which this could be interpreted, one way is to consider the percentage of immigrants that make up the population of a country. In this regard, immigrants represent 37% of the entire population in Saudi Arabia, 88.4% in the United Arab Emirates, 28.8% in Australia, 33.3% in Jordan, 75.5% in Kuwait, 39.1% in Hong Kong, 46% in Singapore and 29.6% in Switzerland (Migration Policy Institute, 2017).

Finally, it is also important to consider how certain corridors grew particularly between 2000 and 2017 based on UN data. During this time, North America was one of the fastest growing destinations for migrants with origins in Africa (4.9% growth annually over this time) while at the same time, the number of African-born migrants heading to Asia increased by around 4.2% annually (UN Report, 2017: 13). Asian-born immigrants increased by 2.6% per year in Oceania and 2.6% per year in North America. In this time period, there was also an increase in the percentage of people born in Europe immigrating to Africa (3.5% per year) while North American-born immigrants residing in Latin America and the Caribbean also increased (3.1% per year). These 'returns' may indicate that migrants who had children abroad are now coming back to their 'home' countries.

For scholars who focus explicitly on the consequences of such mobility, migration impacts our understanding of society broadly, and people and differences specifically. In the context of migration, there exists the possibility that societies will change to accommodate differences through their economic institutions, cultural scripts, and political formations. Societies have the capacity to learn from the arrivals and encounters taking shape by way of organizations—in other words, organizations play a crucial role in being sites and spaces of encounters between different kinds of people. They can contribute to the ways of being and belonging that people actively pursue through their work, workplaces and other affiliated organizational contexts. In this sense, organizations are central to the ways in which society organizes various forms of work. Any change at the level of society will ultimately include the ways in which people organize socio-cultural, economic, and political dimensions of our lives. This involves organizations as they have been the predominant way in which we have organized the various kinds of work that are necessary for societies to take shape, become replicated, and sustained. The world of organizations broadly and the world of work specifically represents opportunities for changing the ways society has functioned. Moreover, it opens up possibilities for rethinking the form and location of society— does migration allow re-organization of the very forms of society? And in addressing this issue, what role do organizations play in contributing to the form, function, and location of society through the organization of labor and work?

In many nations around the world, the coming together of different people has become the new norm, albeit such 'mixings' are never without tensions, conflict, and contestations. It is likely that the incoming and settling of culturally different 'Others' causes fracturing and the formation of ethnic (or racial, religious) boundaries. Rather than arise as negotiated spaces for new understandings of self, such boundaries are the result of defensive mechanisms and aim to keep certain people out of society. This can happen through the creation of new policies, regulations, and laws aimed to make it more difficult for certain people to access resources, engage in paid labor, or vote. Aimed at limiting who is considered a 'citizen' or who can become a citizen, nation-states ruled or influenced by dominant groups can create new 'rules of the game' as it relates to institutions (North, 1991). In doing so, they aim to keep social, cultural, and political power with contemporary examples in Australia, the US, and the UK as conservative, White (mostly male) leaders and members of society revel in intolerant rhetoric against cultural Others.

Most immediately, the hold on power associated with such groups is central to debates in the US around the Supreme Court nomination of Brett Kavanaugh. The grotesque manner in which hate and privilege intersect underscores the dynamic nature of societies as socio-cultural and political pressures for change and equality (Benhabib, 2002, 2004), such as Black Lives Matter and #MeToo, result in the virulent defense of the status quo. In these instances, what role do organizations play? And how their existing forms and functions potentially replicate racial and ethnic hierarchies despite the patina of mottos, such as 'We are committed to diversity and inclusion' or 'All are welcome'. Rather than offering new opportunities for reorganizing societal functions, could organizations (and the ways in which we have organized work) continue to limit the opportunities and access to resources despite being located in liberal democracies?

Within this context, multiculturalism has been the dominant theoretical framework for examining and speaking about the ways in which the influx of people via migration impacts societies. Yet as this chapter will suggest, multiculturalism as a lens to understand these societal changes is not sufficient. Relying on concepts associated with multiculturalism does not allow consideration for the ways *transnational* aspects of migration have impacted societies, organizations, and work. Rather, new ideas around differences are necessary particularly in the context of organizations and work. Transnational migration studies offers both critiques of the existing ways in which multiculturalism has been deployed in MOS and alternative ways to examine these issues. If the previous three chapters were engaged in a discussion around the new ways people and difference can be studied via the notion of subjectivity, the focus in the next three chapters broadens the possibilities for the MOS scholarship in attending to the intersections of difference and work. They do so by expanding the scope of possibilities and contributions from transnational migration studies.

This chapter examines critically the concept of multiculturalism and then moves onto to specifically focus on the ways in multiculturalism has been conceptualized and used in MOS literature. It outlines how these approaches replicate problematic assumptions related to culture, race/ethnicity and belonging, and finishes with new ideas on culture and difference by way of transnational migration studies in the context of MOS scholarship. It offers new directions for studying differences in the context of organizational scholarship by providing contextual depth to the ways difference has been individualized in the MOS literature.

Multiculturalism in question

Multiculturalism can be defined as the co-existence of culturally different people in modern societies with and without histories of migration. The defining factor for such a condition is the multiplicity of different cultures existing within the same society and, hence, nation-state. Given that the existence of multiculturalism is based on the concept of culture, defining and understanding culture is an important dimension for expanding on it in the form of multiculturalism. Yet defining culture is an epistemic, ethical, and political act: it requires delineating a set of worldviews, social relationships, practices, and people as belonging together in a society and nation-state while at the same time, and by way of omission, suggesting that others are *not* part of a particular culture, society, and nation-state. In other words, culture is an affirmation of certain people who are theorized as belonging (together) and a simultaneous disavowal of others who are theorized as outsiders.

The cultural paradigm used to differentiate people has its roots in the colonial disciplinary gaze of anthropology but has also become the mainstay of other contemporary social science disciplines including sociology, cultural studies, and MOS. The cultural paradigm results in a 'container concept of society' (Wimmer and Glick Schiller, 2002) and subsumes difference under the celebratory notion of multiculturalism despite the fact that multiculturalism is inherently a conversation about the 'politics of recognition' (Taylor, 1994). The culture part of multiculturalism is a meaning-giving system that transcodes, rearticulates, and reconstructs signifying elements (Hall, 2017/1994) and thereby produces particular subjects, such as Asian, White, Black, and so forth, while at the same it attempts to limit the varieties of subjects (Bakhtin, 1977) that can exist.

Race and other forms of differences as exemplified through multiculturalism are the products of a 'hierarchical system that produces differences' (Hall, 2017/1994: 33). Hall (2017/1994: 20–21) suggests that the 'return' of multiculturalism as the 'proliferation of hyphenated identities as a celebratory affirmation of difference' is a hallmark preoccupation in liberal democracies whereby individuals are expected to give up particularistic attachments in favor of 'civic rationality based on universalist principles'. When used in this sense, *multiculturalism functions as an ethico-political epistemology of naming and knowing people*. It provides the symbolic frames for making sense of people and difference but occludes historic and institutionalized structures that privilege some people over others. People come into being through the axioms of difference the moment they are named as subjects of a multicultural society. The moment migrant people become known as multicultural subjects marks their disappearance from any other narrative possibility or subjectivity: they are known only in the ways, words, and language of multiculturalism.

In effect, their histories of arrival, practices of transnational being and belonging, and contemporary subjectivities become effaced under the terms of multiculturalism. If hyphenation marks the death of the migrant subject, then the hyphen is an apt gravestone to note the site of such death as the in-between. Multiculturalism classifies whole groups of people, leaving little to no room for ambiguity or liminality. As a concept, it devours and remakes people's lives, sense of self and sense of the world so as to fit into existing notions of society. Racial and ethnic ambiguity challenges the very foundations of multiculturalism given its additive nature: people are seen as the sum of various cultural elements with little opportunity to be something else or different. In the context of liberal democracies, notions of power and privilege are left unattended as multiculturalism is seen as the solution to 'the problem of living with difference' (Hall, 2017/1994: 86). Yet not all societies and nation-states are liberal democracies: what about those instances in which cultural mixings take shape through different histories of being and belonging?

As the copious amounts of data presented in the start of this chapter indicate, migration between different nation-states in Asia constitutes the largest mobility of people in the world. For example, the current movement of Chinese mainlanders to Hong Kong reminds us of the political project that is taking shape through such activities. As Hong Kong becomes a full-fledged part of China in the coming years, the institutions and ways of being and belonging that came to be during British rule will undoubtedly change. In such instances, multiculturalism (as a concept) and the various transnational subjectivities that have emerged may be seen as threatening to the One China policy of Beijing. Thus, political aspirations may curtail and even outlaw the ability of people to identify themselves in previous ways. In such cases, the social world becomes reconstructed due to state intervention and thereby, certain subjectivities may become too disruptive or dangerous to hegemonic narratives of nation. Already, the shutting down of Hong Kong National Party due to Beijing's demands has signaled that previous modes of organizing will no longer be tolerated given they represent free speech and democracy (Kuo, 2018). Within this context, more social, cultural, and political curtailing will likely follow, signaling that difference can be deemed as a serious threat to national and global politics.

Thus, understanding the context and conditions under which multiculturalism may be seen as disruptive is quite relevant for its critique. In this sense, the critique of multiculturalism in the context of China/ Hong Kong is not based on its inadequacy in speaking to new kinds and forms of subjectivities emerging out of mobility but, rather, for its potential to disrupt nation-building efforts. These considerations are, to some extent, different than the ways in which multiculturalism is used as a mechanism to control difference in liberal democracies. It is imperative to understand how migration and mobility across national borders impact narratives for understanding and rethinking multiculturalism: as a disruptive force, as a control mechanism, as a professed tool for integration. And if multiculturalism can be both disruptive and a control mechanism, what alternatives are there to rethinking difference? Here, speaking about ideology and intention becomes quite relevant in the sense that such concepts are powerful in as much as they replicate or resist hegemonic ideas of selfhood, nationhood, and belonging. Difference can be seen as quite threatening to existing orders, aspirant nationhood, and fantasies of community.

As a point of contrast, transnational migration provides new subjectivities and concepts that intervene in multiculturalism as the narrative for personhood and nationhood in post-migration liberal democracies. This is important given that notions of race, ethnicity, and other forms of difference that represent the ways societies are organized in the Western context do not necessarily have epistemological equivalents in other contexts. Moreover, such subjectivities allow consideration for resistance to state narratives, dominant ideologies, and socio-cultural norms. In these instances, speaking back as a transmigrant, hybrid, or cosmopolitan to pre-determined notions and narratives of multiculturalism can be possible. The possibility that such subjectivities can become manifestations of resistance must be included in any new theories or theorization about difference and selfhood in MOS—this then is the new way in which we can begin to re-theorize and re-think what multiculturalism is and how it may be used to suppress other narratives of self, nationhood, and belonging.

In addition to resistance, when people move, new forms of difference arise and studying them through extant categories of difference cannot attend to emergent subjectivities. When theories and concepts about diversity and difference travel, they also become something else, something new, and something potentially unrecognizable (Calás et al., 2009). People, ideas, and practices are all mobile subjects in the sense that their movement can be studied through research. It is important to consider when, why, and how subjects move and the conditions under which mobility is undertaken. Multiculturalism does not and cannot attend to these mobilities as it only offers a hyphen and limited choices for 'identities' on arrival. The continuation of a person's journey, their narratives and practices of being and belonging in a transnational mode are left unattended through the language and lens of multiculturalism.

In contrast, new subjectivities arising from transnational migration studies—transmigrants, hybrids and cosmopolitans—challenge not only the ways in which societies name people but also ahistoric notions of nationhood, extant politico-legal arrangements, and economic systems. For example, transmigrants speak to the ways in which people define themselves in agentic and reflexive ways including in the context of work. These behaviors and practices can be seen not only as affirming something but also as resisting the personhood imposed on them by multiculturalism as the *only* narrative of being and belonging. In this sense, transnational subjectivity is about resistance and resisting dominant forms of knowing people. It is a counter-hegemonic move in the same domain of the ethico-epistemic and political as multiculturalism.

Similarly, hybridity is not simply about new mixings but also a conversation about power: who is *allowed* to mix with whom and under what circumstances. As Coombes and Brah (2000) suggest, hybridity is a concept that needs to be understood in the context of race relations and discourses, and practices of miscegenation taking shape in different societies. Hybridity speaks (back) to those notions of racial purity, European or Western progress, and race-based classifications of people as superior (White) or inferior (Black, Brown, Asian) in making possible such subjectivities in society and at work. Finally, cosmopolitan addresses not only the emergence of reflexive orientations toward the world but also the agentic and ethical aspects of work. Altogether, the subjectivities arising from transnational migration studies take shape through epistemic, social, and material practices across transnational social fields and in a multiscalar fashion.

Doing multiculturalism after mobility

While there are efforts to speak about organizational efforts that can lead to inclusion of multicultural individuals in organizations (Trefry, 2006; Halverson and Tirmizi, 2008; Lauring and Selmer, 2012), the epistemology of multiculturalism in diversity research first makes people 'knowable' or 'subjects' through existing categories and constructs, and second, once they are known, focuses on how best to manage them through organizational practices and policies. In this sense, integration and assimilation still dominate multiculturalism discourses and modes of analysis in diversity research as they relate to Otherness in terms of race, gender, ethnicity, culture, and so forth. With notable exceptions that attend to power relations (Ragins, 1997), one of the main aims of diversity research is to provide solutions to best integrate certain groups, such as women and minorities, into organizational contexts through various management practices, such as mentoring and sponsorship, or inclusion-focused human resources policies.

As Liu (2016a, 2016b) suggests, diversity management can be the manifestation of Whiteness in organizations whereby power relations are kept intact under the guise of multiculturalism. Within this context, discourses of integration and accommodation occlude dialogue about the ontological status of the subject of diversity and why they need to 'fit' or assimilate in the first place. Diversity research as a reflection of such multiculturalism brings about epistemic closure to the kinds of selves that are possible in organizations without consideration of how the very structuring of structures in organizations delimit who can occupy which positions: a concern about diversity, inclusion *and* belonging. The myopic focus on 'best practices for diversity and inclusion' does not address power relations and, therefore, cannot attend to the production and perpetuation of inequalities in organizational contexts (DiTomaso et al., 2007; Zanoni et al., 2010; Berry and Bell, 2012; Berrey, 2014; Tomaskovic-Devey, 2014; Williams et al., 2014), some of which are the result of the very practices adopted for diversity and inclusion (Kalev et al., 2006; Liu, 2016b).

Within the context of diversity research, the study of multiculturalism after migration must attend to the way in which discourses of difference take shape within power structures both inside and outside organizations. This can only be accomplished if there is a clear understanding of history and context. For example, how do the very notions and discourses of difference become exemplified in contemporary societies? What kinds of people occupy what kinds of jobs in societies? And how do the ways in which work is organized reflect broader societal patterns of inequality or how does such organizing of work continue to replicate the inequalities?

Shared legacies of colonialism, imperialism, slavery, and other historic forms of oppression have laid the foundations, albeit differently, for many modern-day nations and societies. In these contexts, people make sense and meaning in their lives through multiscalar practices that ascribe work and organizational experiences certain status and relevance in the production of transnational selves.

To this end, multiculturalism in diversity research exemplifies an epistemic subsuming when derived from psychological and cultural constructs based on Western individualism (Özkazanç-Pan and Calás, 2015). By depoliticizing race/ethnicity, diversity research results in the erasing of history and of *becoming* when people are conceptualized through notions of race and ethnicity that are disembodied from the bodies, practices, and ideas that give them significance. Ressia et al. (2017) address this issue through intersectionality as they examine the job-seeking experiences of non-English speakers in Australia—as such, histories of (be)coming are relevant to any conversation around workplace 'fit'. Consequently, attending to multiculturalism from a transnational lens requires discussion about the nature of society and historic transformations beyond the individual or group in question. Without doing this kind of work, research cannot answer questions around why migrants are still asked to 'fit in' to workplaces despite the value they bring based on their experiences.

On this topic, Guo and Al Ariss (2015) suggest that human resource management (HRM) practices need to understand the value associated with migrants' experiences as they relate to skills in the workplace. Mahadevan and Kilian-Yasin (2017) call on scholars to engage in reflexive HRM research that does not Orientalize or marginalize subjects, such as Muslim migrants in the context of Germany. Critically oriented work speaks to the silence on and about power relations in research that examines culturally different others (Primecz et al., 2016). In all, these works from within the field of cross-cultural management specifically, and diversity more broadly, raise issues around how the subject of research is conceptualized. While concurring with their observations in general, the intention of this book is to propose ways to move beyond such limited critique. In other words, new subjectivities and subjects of research on differences in the context of work are necessary in order to attend to the very issues around marginalization, Orientalism, and other silencing mechanisms that take shape in research that claims to attend to difference.

In order to move beyond existing approaches and critiques, it is imperative to address history and context as they impact how people engage in their epistemic, social, and material practices of *being* and *belonging*. Transnational is not simply an adjective for a kind of migrant but rather it is ontology: it reorients how we think about the social world and the ways we engage with it/in it. As a consequence, any examination of multiculturalism and its potential 'benefits' in an organizational context or workplace must also attend to the broader economic arrangements, such as capitalism. The extractive nature of capitalism becomes embodied in organizational scholarship when people are seen as sources of labor and differentiated based on their skills and experiences. This integration perspective in HRM (Hajro, 2017; Hajro, Zilinskaite, and Stahl, 2017) and diversity research (Hajro, Gibson and Pudelko, 2017) embodies this assumption as it attempts to clearly articulate the best ways such migrants can be utilized and assimilated into existing organizational systems. If we follow this approach to its epistemological foundation, then culture and multiculturalism are valuable to the extent that migrants' (and other groups) *different* cultural repertoires, based on their experiences and worldviews, are deemed useful to the organization's goals. Yet in order to become useful to organizational ends, such people need to go through a process of assimilation via diversity management—an approach that attempts to efface extant relations of difference and power to achieve non-threatening forms of difference.

While a person may experience privilege in particular contexts based on their gender, race, or any other relations of difference, the same individual may experience marginalization in another context based on these same relations. For example, Brubaker (2013) demonstrates how 'Muslim' is both as a category of analysis and a social, political, and religious practice that can be used to understand different migrant experiences in various European nations. In this sense, multiculturalism after migration speaks to how different forms and ways of becoming and belonging take shape in different contexts inclusive of the different subjectivities outlined in previous chapters. It is a conversation about historic power relations, economic structures that may advantage certain groups over others, and cultural formations that ascribe particular attributes to people in the context of the 'nation'. Multiculturalism in the context of diversity research must attend to historic formations and their present-day manifestations in relation to the possibilities of subjectivity: what kinds of selves are possible for whom and under what conditions in organizations?

To this end, the subjectivities discussed previously arise out of societal changes in relation to multiculturalism, conceptualized as:

> a demographic description, a broad political ideology, a set of
> specific public policies, a goal of institutional restructuring,
> a mode of resourcing cultural expression, a general moral

> challenge, a set of new political struggles, and as a kind of
> feature of postmodernism. (Vertovec, 2001: 3)

Yet when diversity research attends to multiculturalism, it does so as an add-on to an existing self such that the multicultural self is understood as the result of identifying with more two sets of cultural and, to an extent, political values. Despite their aims to offer insights into the complexity of multicultural people and their experiences, such approaches neither attend to power dimensions of race and ethnicity as they relate to multiculturalism nor to the structural inequalities that people with and without migrant histories face in their lives and work settings among other organizations.

In all, new conversations about multiculturalism in MOS are necessarily derived from the emergent subjectivities. Yet it is not only that there are new forms of selfhood arising and emerging out the historic and contemporary encounter of people that needs attention but rather considerations around who is moving where, why, and under what conditions. The data on migration points to clear bilateral corridors but it also points to new ways in which migrant labor power is building economies in different parts of the world. Despite being unable to vote, have a say in their working conditions and salaries, and suffer human rights violations (such as the South Asian migrant workers in the Middle East), migrant workers are creating new societies. Multiculturalism does not attend to the power relations and differences when it 'celebrates' differences rather than attend to the ways those differences are constructed and how inequalities travel transnationally. It is necessary but not sufficient to attend to the new subjectivities of transmigrants, hybrids, and cosmopolitans as bearers of difference but rather they must be contextualized specifically in relation to migrant work inclusive of its conditions—such as the working conditions of migrant domestic care workers in Europe (Lutz, 2016) or the transnational lives of migrant farm workers (McLaughlin et al., 2017).

Altogether, these and many other examples point to the fact that multiculturalism must be reexamined not as a conceptual container for all the difference we see in societies but rather as a product of various moments in history. In Western liberal democracies, this term speaks to specific historical attempts to integrate cultural Others, including those from former colonies (such as in France and the UK). In other contexts, the term may be seen as a threat to nation-building efforts. Still, in other contexts and nations, it might be contested to consider whose culture is recognized in multiculturalism efforts—for example, in the context of Latin America, race and genes are part of any conversation around culture, a highly politicized and polarizing concept (Daniel, 2018). Yet in the context of MOS, multiculturalism is still considered an additive approach to having more than two cultures as points of identification. The psychological dimensions of this concept still dominate much of the literature. As a consequence, the rich context, history, power relations, and nationhood efforts as part of this concept are rarely addressed in theories about people and difference.

By acknowledging the very ways in which multiculturalism has become a dominant narrative for speaking about difference in MOS, the ways in which we theorize difference can be expanded. Moreover, we can begin to acknowledge that the construction of this concept is based in a particular moment in Western history: how to include and account for non-White people whose histories, and ways of being and belonging do not mirror existing ones. Multiculturalism as a concept, as a practice, and as a narrative of being and belonging in a transnational mode becomes challenged: the epistemic, social, and material practices we associate with being multicultural in the West or in particular liberal democracies do not travel, translate, or occupy the same position in other contexts or nations. It is this 'unfitting' into existing categories that is the hallmark of a transnational migration studies contribution: ways of being and belonging that make sense in one context do not necessarily exist or make sense in others. By opening up epistemological space to see/theorize these rather than obscure them through existing ideas and theories, we may just be able to re-theorize MOS in a transnational mode. Yet to accomplish this means to constantly question the underlying values and assumptions guiding extant theories about 'cultural Others' and difference with the aim of dismantling existing categories of identifying and differentiating people in the world. When the world moves, our theories must also be able to move. As of yet, the field of MOS has yet to move with the world in order to understand how its ways of theorizing may be limiting rather than expanding what is considered knowledge about diversity, difference, and culture.

To build further upon these ideas and critiques, the next chapter focuses explicitly on inequality. One of the defining features of our contemporary era is that of growing inequalities across a variety of dimensions. Yet can and does MOS theorizing when it speaks about culture and difference attend to the ways in which inequalities are taking shape? And moreover, does it examine the ways organizations and the ways in which work has been organized globally contribute to the growing inequalities faced by many migrant workers? In examining and addressing these questions in the next chapter, the goal is to center inequality into any analysis of transnationalism in the context of organizational analysis.

Inequalities on the Move

The previous chapter focused on one of the new ways in which transnational migration studies inform the field of management and organization studies vis-à-vis the theorization and study of difference beyond the level of people. In this regard, the ways in which multiculturalism as a concept and practice have been studied and deployed in the MOS field were critiqued and new considerations offered for a nuanced and contextualized approach to its adoption. This chapter builds on novel ways the field of MOS can move forward in attending to difference by considering the notion of inequalities. That is, how inequalities take shape in the context of organizations and due to organizations, and the various ways in which such inequalities exist in multi-levels in societies among other considerations. To understand the relevance of inequalities for the study of difference, this chapter focuses on three elements.

The first is an examination of how individual experiences around inequality need to be brought to the forefront of any research on diversity, difference, and cross-cultural experiences. In other words, the ways in which inequalities take shape in the context of one's particular positionality and in relation to organizational experiences need further examination. While these issues have been considered to a larger extent in other social science fields, such as sociology, anthropology, and geography, they have yet to impact management and organization studies in a substantial way. In many ways, the study of inequalities can sometimes become overly focused on 'perceptions' of justice in organizations, such as the oft-deployed procedural or distribute justice aspects of organizational behavior research (see Rupp et al., 2017, for an overview), and their relationship to employee behaviors or organizational outcomes. Rather, the focus on inequalities arriving from transnational migration studies will expand on this rather narrow and individualist (and relative) notion of 'justice' and 'fairness'. In fact, the ways in which inequalities take shape through intentional and nonintentional acts in particular organizations need to be examined in considering the embedded nature of organizations in relation to their socio-cultural, political, and economic contexts. Thus, history, context, and structural considerations beyond the individual must be part of any analysis on inequalities and people.

The second area of focus in the chapter will be on the transnational modes through which inequalities travel. In other words, inequalities that have a particular form in one context may not exist in the same form when they 'arrive' in another context. As Calás et al. (2009) note, there has been little consideration of the ways in which diversity relates to inequalities globally and few socio-historical analyses to provide insights around the production of diversity as a field of inquiry and practice. Meanwhile, examples of research on transnational relationships in relation to subject formations, inequalities, and professional identities (for example, see Butcher, 2009; Durr, 2011; Erdal and Oeppen, 2013) exist beyond MOS and cross-cultural management. In all, the allure of identity has shifted focus away from the inequality dimension of organizations (Michaels, 2016) and, as such, most existing research in relation to difference focuses on identity dimensions rather than consider the ways in which inequities develop, diffuse and reassemble across scales.

The third area will focus on the ways in which diversity work, such as diversity training, cross-cultural sensitivity training and other forms of difference-bridging work, do not voice or challenge extant inequalities that gave rise to the need for such work in the first place. Ahmed's (2016) notion of diversity work as 'making others comfortable with the fact of your arrival' resonates with questions of belonging both in society and in organizational contexts. By examining why 'diversity work' in organizations continues to be necessary in the context of multicultural societies, we can begin to address the very assumptions about difference, power relations and inequalities that drive scholarly diversity research. As suggested by Ahonen and Tienari (2015), diversity research and its attendant knowledge claims are not neutral scholarship. In light of this, future diversity scholarship requires an ethical commitment to tracing the formation of multiscalar inequalities inclusive of organizational practices and policies that may be producing and/or replicating them. Thus, the mobility turn in social sciences is not a celebratory one to suggest that everyone moves but, rather, a serious engagement with the interrelated relations of power, inequality, and dispossession taking shape in a multiscalar fashion as people move either out of choice, force, or need in relation to work and organizations (see Mai, 2013, on global sex workers).

In all, this chapter opens up possibilities for engaging with inequalities as a necessary and important conversation that is part of diversity and cross-cultural research—any scholarship attending to difference must also attend to the ways such differences are emblematic of historic and ongoing societal power relations between and among different kinds of people. Such power relations often have racial and gender dimensions and the focus in this book has been on race/ethnicity rather than gender. This is an important consideration in that any future scholarship must build on these foundations to uncover the complexity of transnational experiences and encounters beyond race/ethnicity—concepts that may or may have epistemological equivalents in non-White societies as people differentiate themselves in other ways.

Perceptions of fairness or inequality light

One of the most prominent ways in which ideas related to equity, fairness, and justice make their way into organizational scholarship is through psychological constructs, such as procedural and distributive justice (Lind and Tyler, 1988; Pinder, 2014). Most often, research aims to determine whether employees 'feel' or 'perceive' their organization in general, organizational practices, process, and policies specifically as fair. The research generally then goes on to examine what happens in organizations where employees feel/perceive a higher degree of fairness versus a lower degree (McFarlin and Sweeney, 1992; Proudfoot and Lind, 2015). In all, the consideration is around the ways in which perceptions of fairness and justice impact employee behavior, team outcomes, and ultimately the success of the organization. There is little examination or consideration of the ways in which fairness and justice are the result of epistemic, social, and material practices rather than mere perceptions of individuals.

Yet by coding fairness and justice as individual level psychological attributions made in relation to a particular set of organizational processes, practices, and policies, organizational scholarship is unable to attend to inequalities. Rather, perceptions of fairness and justice become the dominant form of any discussion in the domain of equality. The language of fairness and justice obstructs considerations around the structuring of jobs, organizations, and society more broadly in terms of whose work and labor is deemed valuable and whose work and contributions remain invisible, unrecognized, and under/unvalued. And who or what are seen as threats to fairness and justice in organizations? In other words, are people who suggest they are experiencing unfairness or injustice simply those who have different perceptions? Given the dominance of psychological constructs as the driver of conversations on this topic, there is little opportunity to move beyond the mind.

As a consequence, organizational behavior literature becomes void of critical considerations around inequality in organizations given its focus on individual perceptions. This approach results in attempts to measure justice and fairness in organizations (Colquitt and Rodell, 2015) rather than an approach that focuses on historic and contemporary inequalities such as labor force segmentation (Alt and Iversen, 2017) and job stratification (Baron and Bielby, 1980; Adam Cobb, 2016) and the experiences of these inequalities by various employee segments. Thus, the perceptions may be based on historic and contemporary realities related to cultural and racial hierarchies in organizations. In fact, research demonstrates that hiring decisions in relation to immigrants are made in a manner that preserves cultural and racial hierarchies in particular organizational contexts (Auer et al., 2016; Ndobo et al., 2017). Moreover, Zambrana et al. (2017) demonstrate that immigrants and minorities experience micro-aggressions and discrimination not as a matter of perception but as actual epistemic, social, and material practices. These practices then result in inequalities related to promotion, value, and recognition in the organization but also reflect broader inequalities in society in relation to the value and recognition placed on immigrants and minorities—at least in the US context. As a point of contrast, the approach to inequalities in MOS is almost nonexistent and differences come into play in a rather comparative way. The examination of differences between employees focuses explicitly on their perceptions of fairness and justice rather than their experiences of injustice, inequality, and unfairness. Difference becomes muted as a psychological construct in how people perceive and understand their work environment rather than the result of historic and ongoing inequalities.

In other words, the MOS field focuses on perceptions of fairness and justice rather than actual inequalities that may lead people to understand their work environments in certain ways. Difference and justice studied in this way forms an uncritical approach that may replicate inequalities rather than uncover and challenge them. If the researchers are looking for differences between and among people in relation to how they understand their work context and organizational experiences, then any examination of differences vis-à-vis people must also attend to inequality as context, as practice, and as historic but also ongoing. In other words, the decontextualizing and individualizing elements of the search for and documenting of differences must no longer be the dominant ways in which diversity and cross-cultural management research operates. Inequality is one of the foremost defining features of societies today— to ignore this in the context of management and organization studies, particularly in relation to the ways such inequalities move and change as they cross scales, places, and spaces, limits the progress of the scholarly field. As one solution, transnational migration studies provides analytic rigor and concepts for the study of mobile inequalities, an issue that is expanded on next.

Mobile inequalities

One of the main drivers of migration is the pursuit of employment in other nations and contexts. Available data on formal employment based on immigration for the US show that in the period between 2007 and 2017, around 3.5 million petitions were filed for employment-based visas and around 80% of those applications were approved (USCIS [H1B petitions filed], 2018). During this period, most beneficiaries (by country of birth) were from India, around 64%, while the remaining top petitioning nations included China, Canada, Philippines, South Korea, the UK and Mexico. In the last three years (2015–17), the top three petitioning firms in the US were Cognizant Tech Solutions, Tata Consultancy Services, and Infosys— all firms with ties to India, in computer-related sectors, and involved in placements in Silicon Valley. For 2017, the average starting salary at these firms was around $82,000 for employees, who were predominantly hired with Bachelor's degrees (USCIS [H1B petitions approved], 2018). In the 2018 fiscal year, males on average accounted for 74% of all petitioners, thus signifying a highly-gender imbalanced approach whereby women account for around 25% of all petitioners. Moreover, around 70% of all petitioners between 2007 and 2017 were between the ages of 25 and 34.

These formal numbers cannot speak to the informal ways in which immigrants may move and find employment that is not 'counted' by official measures. Yet the intersections of labor markets, gender, age and race/ethnicity provide interesting insights, at least in the US case, for considering how the availability of certain elite jobs allows younger males from particular nations the opportunity to move. In turn, these mobilities provide further insights about the interactions of mobilities and inequalities—can mobility prevent inequality? Or does mobility for one group reinforce inequality for others who 'stay'? Transnational migration studies provide analytic tools to consider these issues beyond facing job discrimination in particular contexts—how do inequalities move? Do they change or become something else with each encounter or movement? And are there ways in which resistance can be enacted in relation to inequalities that follow individuals?

Guided by a transnational migration lens, mobility is another dimension of inequality which requires attention and analysis beyond considering the ways in which labor markets and employment opportunities may be truncated or limited for certain groups of individuals in certain contexts. A transnational perspective on inequality opens up opportunities to understand dimensions beyond professional networks of immigrants (such as those highlighted by Saxenian et al., 2002). Rather, transnational modes of analysis allow consideration of three interrelated issues: the arrival of inequalities and their potential circumvention; the movement of particular segments of society as it relates to those 'left behind'; and the ways in which the form and locations of inequalities change across transnational scales.

To expand on this point, the transnational scales perspective allows the examination of the mechanisms and processes through which different and potentially new forms of inequalities emerge through the movement of people. Through ongoing encounters between different people, their practices and ideas, inequalities related to one's position in society and work opportunities may take shape. These new forms of inequalities may include deskilling (Creese and Wiebe, 2012)—highly-educated professionals taking up employment in fields and sectors that require little to no educational attainment—, precarious and contingent work (Milkman, 2013)—gig economy work—, informal work (Portes and Haller, 2010; Arango and Baldwin-Edwards, 2014)—caregiving, factory work—, or illegal work (Webb et al., 2009).

In her research, Shih (2006) examines the networks and job-strategies of White women, Asian men, and Asian women in the context of Silicon Valley. Given the historically White, male dominance in engineering and computer-related fields, particularly in Silicon Valley, Shih (2006: 179) finds that the 'characteristic of job-hopping in the region serves as a useful strategy by which these groups could circumvent employers and firms that they viewed as discriminatory'. In addition, Shih reports, 'the region's reliance on networks did not disadvantage White women, Asian men, and Asian women' (2006: 179). This is counterintuitive because lack of access to key networks has been consistently identified as problematic in studies of work and organizations. However, because of the specific histories of these groups' entrance into Silicon Valley, respondents reported being able to create and tap into resource-rich, cross-rank, gender- and ethnic-based networks that could rival the utility of 'old white boys' networks' (Shih, 2006: 179). While Asian men and women job-hop into firms that are run by co-ethnics, White women navigate jobs by considering employers and firms that are seen as women-friendly.

As an exemplar, this study demonstrates that inequalities are not necessarily stagnant but that they can be mobile. In other words, the ways in which people arrive into organizations and become employees are not necessarily neutral and merit based. Rather, work opportunities themselves are a form of inequality and further exist within a context of inequality. The ways in which organizational opportunities become constrained based on one's race/ethnicity and gender as they move between places, organizations, and contexts is perhaps the most relevant contribution of transnational analysis. Given that many organizations grapple with best practices around diversity and inclusion, it is well worth noting that inequalities are not simply taking shape within one organization but that they are taking shape through organizations—the additive effect of mobile inequalities is that new job-hopping strategies and employment options, such as entrepreneurship, take shape out of necessity rather than choice.

The mobility aspect speaks to the ways in which the problem of discrimination and inequality is not one that is contained only to the workplace but dispersed across societies and scales: what happens when large numbers of males between the ages of 25 and 34 leave India for the US? How do the contexts in which they were embedded change and with what consequences? Their arrival to the US might be celebrated as a form of 'multiculturalism' but the reality is that they face barriers in employment, are not guaranteed the rights that citizens, enjoy and their mobility is dependent (and contingent) on legal, political, economic, and cultural factors. Yet if scholars were to examine such individuals' experiences of work, their work conditions, and workplaces in general, the guiding concepts from diversity and cross-cultural management would likely consider some combination of the following: examining the experiences of perceived justice and/or fairness and relating those perceptions to high-turnover rates for Asian engineers. Alternatively, there could be comparisons between Asian engineers and other engineers in the same organization across race, gender, and team dynamics. And lastly, there could be examinations of how cross-cultural training in the workplace could support the retention and promotion of highly-qualified immigrant laborers. Yet all of these hypothetical approaches that are based on existing frameworks would miss the complexity of the problem: the pervasive and mobile nature of inequalities in a transnational scalar fashion.

As one example, consider the ways in which physicians arriving to the US are unable to practice their profession but must take licensing exams that often onerous and expensive (Peterson et al., 2014). The immobility of human capital then creates inequalities related to professional opportunities, community gaps in healthcare, and physician-deserts across the nation resulting in decreased accessibility. The lack of readily available employment opportunities for highly-trained professionals has specific historic trajectories and contemporary outcomes. While in the technology sector, the mobility of elite, professional workers seems more intentional and dynamic in relation to their initial placement, the arrival of immigrant physicians is met with immediate immobility. This immobility creates a domino and scalar effect on inequalities in the host nation when the human and cultural capital cannot be deployed to support the healthcare needs of immigrants and non-immigrants alike. It creates and continues inequalities in communities that already face barriers to access in healthcare due to bias, language, and culture (for example, see Sarpel et al., 2018, for Chinese communities).

At the same time, mobility refers to those practices and ideas that travel via people, social media, and other platforms and, on arriving, they can become something altogether different and new. One of the reasons particular racial/ethnic communities may benefit little from existing forms of healthcare delivery and practices is that their set of ideas and beliefs related to medicine and health is derived from another context, time, and location—for example, Vietnamese oral health practices and narratives. Based on decades of immigration and place-making, such practices and narratives arrived to the US, continued their influence, and impacted individuals in different ways. On arriving, they became hybrids with Western ideas and health practices, or became the dominant narrative and practice related to oral hygiene while, at other times, they became subsumed under US narratives of oral hygiene and health (see Nguyen et al., 2017). In all, the ways in which particular beliefs and practices manifest in certain people, groups, and communities do not have a path-dependent trajectory. As a consequence, ideas around how to 'deal' with cultural Others with regards to diversity and cross-cultural concepts do not allow consideration of the complexity and ambiguity around the issues.

As one final point related to mobile inequalities, large numbers of workers are embedded in contexts with little or no opportunities for employment, safe working conditions, fair pay/living wages, or adherence to international labor standards (among other concerns). Yet the arrival of such workers to other contexts does not signal a change in the opportunities available to them and, in some cases, the social, economic, and political conditions that greet them on entering a new nation and context may be much worse than what they left 'behind'. Many examples of such groups exist, including South East Asian migrant workers in the Arab Middle East, Chinese migrants in Australia (Fitzgerald, 2007), African migrants in various European nations (Garrido and Codó, 2017) and so forth. In other words, mobile inequalities can speak to those transnational scalar ways in which inequalities transform across scales such that extant frames for analyzing them, such as race, class, and gender, may no longer make sense. Given the dominance of these categories in guiding much of the research in diversity and to an extent, cross-cultural management, understanding how these frames of reference may not exist in the same form across different communities and contexts becomes relevant.

In other words, mobile inequalities form a framework to theorize the ways in which inequalities take form, travel, and appear in contexts beyond their 'origin'. Yet how can we begin to 'see' these various inequalities? Perhaps McDowell's (2008) approach is key here. She suggests that we start by asking different questions about our topics. In the case of migrants, she offers the following as questions to guide analytics that are multi-theoretical and multiscalar:

> [H]ow are connections and practices across spatial scales transformed when the subject being made is a migrant? How are the gendered/classed/racialized identities of migrant workers subject to renegotiation on entering a different space? How do traces of the regulatory structures of 'there' affect being 'here'? How do previous cultural assumptions about gender attributes and capacities, about appropriate tasks for, for example, particular gendered categories, whether in the paid labour market or in other arenas, work out across space and time? (McDowell, 2008: 479)

Thus, theorizing and researching mobile inequalities requires asking a very different set of questions in order for them to become 'visible'. This line of questioning requires contextualizing the research around inequalities but at the same, understanding how they take shape in a transnational fashion. Such an approach requires rethinking the guiding assumptions of research that focuses on difference: research should not be concerned with differences between migrant groups in matters related to organizational outcomes or other decontextualized research inquiries.

The examination of mobile inequalities via new research approaches and questions fundamentally exposes their multiscalar, geographic, institutional, and historic character. This approach, which is derived from transnational migration studies, exposes the complexity of differences in the lived experiences of various groups of migrants as well as the scalar aspect of how inequalities take shape in the first place. Research that adopts such a view can address how migrant deskilling and engagement in precarious work (Lewis et al., 2015) allows Global North cities, like London and New York, to become 'successful' in relation to finance, real estate, and insurance sectors. Immigrant workers in these sectors sustain not only the city but also a neoliberal, capitalist-based economy which continues to exploit workers, particularly economic migrants. Fundamentally, such a research question expands notions of difference in society and organizational experiences beyond diversity dimensions. It takes into account cultural histories and trajectories of 'arriving', institutional and legal structures related to employment, and organizational practices that create an immigrant precarious class and sustain neoliberalism. As a consequence, there will be differences in how such individual view themselves, their employment opportunities and the organizational contexts in which they labor. But naming these differences 'perceptions of justice/fairness' does not adequately capture the broader context in which organizations exist and employees experience work.

New directions in research: inequality as part of the conversation on difference

In much of this book, the guiding principle has been to call attention to the limits of theorizing difference in management and organization studies through critique. Yet some readers may want something more 'affirmative' or some concrete sets of ideas around how to do difference research differently. A conversation on how such research might take shape is well worth addressing; the next chapter on mobile methodologies will address the methods and 'how to' aspects more than will be covered here. Despite the large amount of critique launched in relation to diversity and cross-cultural theories by way of transnational migration studies' concepts, there are also potential new avenues for research. In other words, transnational migration studies offers not only critique of extant approaches and new subjectivities for rethinking how we conceptualize people and differences but it also can provide novel research questions. These questions, in turn, can allow for fundamentally different ways in which we engage in research on/about diversity and culture. Here, I expand on some considerations that can allow for such new directions and, specifically, in terms of how we address and overcome inequality.

One of the main considerations that must be part of any new direction in research attending to differences is to include examination of mobile forms of inequalities that have emerged over time. Transnational migration studies change the conversation on diversity and cross-cultural management to include inequalities in their mobile forms. Given that the mobility ontology guides framework for reconceptualization subjects and subjectivities, the next step is to contextualize the study of such people. To accomplish this, scholars must first look beyond the immediate milieu of organizations and workplaces for their analysis—when the focus is on individuals and/or teams without examining anything outside of the organization, then research ends up being myopic, static, and insular. Scholars should recognize that any observance of difference based on identity categories provides only a static view and is founded on psychological constructs that may not represent the worldviews and experiences of mobile people. Identity-based approaches to understanding difference will not be able to understand the complexity of experiences, practices, and worldviews that emerge under conditions of mobility. Thus, adopting a mobility ontology mean that extant categories and theoretical frameworks must be questioned for appropriateness. Moving on from this, the second step is to consider how to historically contextualize mobile people, practices, and experiences.

Rather, scholars must consider the context of organizations and the ways in which organizations may contribute to existing inequalities, such as furthering neoliberal agendas in the context of various forms of capitalism. Building further on this notion of historic movement is the layering on of historical conjunctures—that is, how do economic factors impact the ways in which mobility happens and the availability of particular employment categories or job opportunities? To examine these issues in depth, scholars should consider these factors and historic societal contexts by way of a mobility lens. Mobility as a guiding ontology is not only about the movement of people but also inequalities. As more nations adopt market economies, transition to capitalist forms of production, or engage in policies aimed at restructuring the economy, opportunities for work will be impacted. These changes will then become impetus for further mobilities as people move in and out of nations to find work. Yet economic changes are not the only reasons mobilities take shape and thus, political, environmental, and cultural factors must also be considered and contextualized in order to understand how various forms of inequalities might be taking shape in a mobile fashion.

For example, any study of differences in the context of work and organizations should also contextualize different subjectivities in relation to narratives of nation and society: how do particular narratives create 'cultural Others' such that the very identity categories used to define and understand people already assumed a particular kind of belonging and citizenship to take shape? At the same time, a researcher should acknowledge that nation-making narratives and practices require the creation of boundaries—who are considered part of the nation and who are considered 'outsiders'. These epistemic, social, and cultural practices must also be understood within the context of political and economic inequalities—who is considered a citizen? What rights do 'non-citizens' have in regard to political representation, employment conditions, and wages? To this end, neither diversity nor cross-cultural management research attend to these broader questions around inequality and whether/how extant research questions may contribute to them when we advise managers on 'how to' deal with diversity and culturally-different employees. Moreover, what about the fact that going global often means organizations perpetuate gendered and racialized employment practices in adverse working conditions in Global South nations (Özkazanç-Pan, 2018)? Rather than holding these conversations under the umbrella of corporate social responsibility (CSR) or ethics, diversity and cross-cultural research must be held accountable for the claims that are made on behalf of cultural Others whose labor is overrepresented in precarious, low-wage work in the US and globally but whose voices are missing from management and organization studies research.

In all, these interrelated research questions provide insights derived from an ontological condition that recognizes mobility as the fundamental condition of the social world. Hence, societal changes and shifts must be included in any analysis that aims to understand why people might have different experiences of work, at work, and in organizational settings generally. Guiding questions related to understanding societal conditions might include the following: what does multiculturalism look like in the particular context? What does citizenship and belonging look like? And how have particular groups of people arrived in this context and/or been associated with certain ideas, practices, and beliefs? Within this context, rather than relying on static notions to identify individuals and then differentiate between them in the context of work, consider the following: how do people continue to make and remake their subjectivities through epistemic, social, and material practices that are transnational and scalar? And how do these practices take shape in workplaces and organizations and with what consequences?

For example, non-binary genders were a defining feature of Native American communities until the advent of Western interventions and forced gender roles (see Hollimon, 2006). Thus, it is imperative to contextualize ways how such historic material and epistemic violence resulted in contemporary social, economic, and political inequalities including those related to employment and work experiences. Without this historic analysis that looks at the arrival of White settlers, narratives of nation, and the formation of inequalities that continue to today, it is difficult to understand the complexity of the Native American experience in work and contemporary organizations. While this is just one example, many more are possible when the research questions, analytic frameworks, and methods are derived from a mobility ontology and guided by concepts from transnational migration studies.

In all, this chapter has focused on the ways that research on diversity and cross-cultural management or difference conceptualized more broadly must include inequality as part of the conversation and research agenda. The idea of mobile inequalities introduced in this chapter allows consideration for the ways in which inequalities take shape, travel, and become potentially something else or different in various contexts. Thus, rigid categories of analysis, such as those derived from identity work, cannot account for or theorize the complexity of experiences and epistemic, social, and material practices that allow for the creation of transmigrant, hybrid, and cosmopolitan subjectivities in the context of mobile inequalities. In other words, mobile inequalities must be included as part of any research agenda that aims to speak about/for differences in a world on-the-move. In the next chapter, mobile methodologies are introduced in order to provide researchers and scholars with concrete tools to engage in research that can attend to mobile subjectivities and transnationalism.

8

Mobile Methodologies

The focus in the previous chapters has been on the new ways to think about broad societal concepts and issues in the context of diversity and cross-cultural research. Namely, the focus was on multiculturalism and mobile inequalities as two equally important and relevant topics that need to be critically unpacked but also reimagined in terms of their relevance for diversity and culture research. In contrast to these more theoretical discussions, this chapter offers discussion in relation to ethics, epistemology, and methodology. To engage scholars that might want to know how to go about doing research guided by mobility, the chapter provides some concrete examples and perspective related to the appropriate methodologies that can guide research in a transnational mode. These examples are provided to offer different ways transnational research can take shape. At the same time, the chapter delves into shared aspects of what might be seemingly very different methodologies and use of methods in these various examples. In all, the chapter aims to provoke questions around what considerations and approaches are necessary in order to carry out research guided by transnational migration studies frameworks.

For example, guided by an ontology of mobility, what new considerations and expectations are there in relation to methodology or the theory of methods? Furthermore, how can scholars study mobile objects/subjects of study when the very methods of social science are guided by static ontologies and generally place-based? And how do notions of ethics and epistemology contribute to rethinking about methodology as the theory of methods? This chapter aims to provide insights to these issues and questions, and also to provide examples based on empirical work across different academic disciplines. In doing so, the goal is to provide multiple ways to engage transnationalism and mobility in thinking about and crafting appropriate methodology. This chapter contributes and, moreover, to our ability to see the ways in which multiscalar global ways of being and belonging take shape. This approach and discussion allow consideration of how adopting particular sets of approaches, methods, and maneuvers can allow the examination of transnationalism in relation to subjectivities, practices, and ideas among other objects/subjects that may exist in a transnational fashion. To accomplish this goal, the chapter is broken up into three sections.

The first section delves into questions and concerns around the theory of methods or methodology under transnational assumptions. The guiding questions in this section are: What difference does transnationalism make to methodology and methods? And what constitutes mobile methodologies? The discussion on these points is followed by examples from empirical work that showcase different ways transnational methods can manifest in social science research. By drawing on examples that cross disciplinary boundaries to examine, highlight, and understand transnational aspects of lives, experiences, and practices among others, this section provides specific methods that can be deployed in transnational research. The final section focuses on how transnational research and mobile methodologies remake the ways in which research on/about difference can be undertaken if it is guided by a transnational migration studies framework. It provides new directions for scholars and scholarship in diversity and cross-cultural management research in the context of ongoing mobilities and globally-connected contexts.

The mobility distinction: methodologies that move

Transnational approaches contribute a multiscalar understanding and analysis of mobile subjectivities such that attending them to them requires moving beyond comparative lenses (Baubock and Faist, 2010; Faist, 2010). They require 'reclassifying existing data, evidence, and historical and ethnographic accounts that are based on bounded or bordered units so that transnational forms and processes are revealed' (Khagram and Levitt, 2007: 2). On this point, Castles (2012) suggests that we see migration as part of or contributing to all social processes rather than an exception. In this regard, migrations including transnational versions speak to the ways in which social transformations are taking shape. Rather than considering how migration contributes to social transformations or vice versa, Castles (2012) suggests examining the ways in which both phenomena inform each other—a far cry from cause/effect and hypothesis testing approaches which delimit the kinds of questions that are asked in the context of transnational migration.

Another consideration is an examination of how various social transformations, such as multiculturalism, inequalities, and other structural and material shifts that result in differential experiences for people, can and should be theorized. Castles states that migration impacts methodology such that it requires

> reflecting on the nature of processes of contemporary social transformation, and including in our analytic models such as key trends as neo-liberal globalization (and the resulting growth in inequality); the increasing economic, political and cultural integration of local communities and national societies into cross-border interactions; and the growth of transnationalism as a form of human agency. (Castles, 2012: 17)

For migration scholars, understanding the role of methodology in addressing and highlighting these issues is crucial to documenting and analyzing the substantive and relative changes taking shape in relation to social transformations. Beyond understanding, it is imperative that scholars devote time to understand how to deploy the right methods guided by their methodology and consider which set of research questions to ask.

As societies change through broad and dynamic social, cultural, economic, political, and technological forces, the impacts of such shifts are felt on a localized and even personal level. The ways in which these factors become relevant in the day-to-day lives, practices, and organizational experiences of individuals must be rendered visible through methodology, inclusive of research questions, design, and methods. This requires asking questions that are derived from an epistemology of transnationalism and trying to understand the significance and role of particular social, epistemic, and material practices for individuals. As the final section of this chapter will demonstrate, these questions can be brought to bear on MOS research in the context of diversity, cross-cultural management, and difference research, broadly defined.

Given the complex and interrelated social, scalar, and spatial dimensions of transnational lives and subjectivities, mobile methodologies refer to various research questions, design and methods attributes of a study that allow scholars to attend to these scalar experiences simultaneously. Rather than one set of definite methods, mobile methodology speaks to those multiple approaches that are brought to bear on the phenomenon in order to provide a comprehensive understanding in the context of mobile subjects/objects of study. This suggests that scholars must be able to bring together several different modes of 'seeing' and doing the research that can range from quantitative to qualitative to mixed methods. Quantitative and data-driven approaches can allow examination of the broader shifts taking place in the context of society, such as employment, movement of people, wages, or other numbers-based ways to provide insights about large scale and historic shifts. At the same time, qualitative approaches can elucidate micro-level strategies, practices, and experiences of transnational modes of working and living that are crucial to the creation of new subjectivities.

Taken together, these distinct approaches and methods create a holistic framework whereby scholars are able to contextualize micro-level observations of social, epistemic and material practices relative to macro-level shifts across the globe. By taking such an approach, scholars can study novel power relations, new ways to engage in citizenship, changes in human and social capital as they relate to work experiences and opportunities and the creation of new transnational ties and networks among many other emergent and dynamic aspects of day-to-day lives. This approach allows an embodied, contextualized and historically-grounded approach that does not decouple broader societal transformations that may seem at a distance from any one individual but still impact, albeit differentially, the local realities and possibilities for immigrant communities. By studying 'differences' in such a way, scholars can being to decipher how and why different individuals and communities embody, engage and practice transnational formations differently— mobile methodologies provide insights as to the different experiences of migration, culture, and belonging; the formation of transnational connections and emergent transnational subjectivities; and practices in relation to organizing/organizational life.

In sum, deploying mobile methodologies requires fundamentally shifting the guiding assumptions of research as based on movement, deriving research questions guided by an epistemology of transnational modes of inquiry, and deploying methods that can attend simultaneously to the macro and micro dimensions of societal shifts. In the next section, examples of research deploying mobile methodologies provide clear opportunities for crafting fieldwork guided by transnational migration studies.

Examples of mobile methods in use

To clarify, a transnational paradigm does not discount the importance of the nation-state but instead holds it as a precarious achievement and construction made possible by discourses of difference and belonging. Yet the nation-state, and thus 'cultural values' as reflections of nation-states, cannot be the starting point for an analysis that aims to understand subjectivities that move across scales and the specificity of experiences associated with encounters. Examples of work that attend to these issues deploy mobile methodologies such that researchers move with the research object/subject over time, place and space as needed to understand the assembling of transnational lives, experiences, and practices.

On the surface, this approach may seem like a multi-sited ethnography (Marcus, 1995) but, unlike traditional ethnographies where sites are physical locations albeit differentially located, transnational fieldwork traces the movements of its object/subject of study. In this sense, the approach is guided by an ontology that is founded on mobility as the fundamental condition of human life and experience. While issues of ontology are rarely spoken about in contemporary management and organization studies research, the assumptions guiding research are well worth voicing in order to understand why particular approaches may or may not be appropriate for studying transnational domains. As a consequence, it is relevant to consider what makes an ontology derived from a mobility condition different than one derived from an understanding that the world is static. Fundamentally, many researchers might agree that the world is generally on the move and things are changing in relation to technology, culture, society, and organizations. This is evidenced through rhetoric and research on the topic of globalization as a phenomenon speaking to the ways the world is becoming 'more connected'. Yet despite the potential agreement about the changing nature of the world and attempts to study it through the lens of globalization, little is being done in the management and organization studies field to bring theories and frameworks derived from a mobility ontology.

Rather, the methods deployed in much of the research examining differences rely on comparisons between established identity categories or cultural scripts—these categories that are relied on to differentiate between and among people are derived from theories that do not recognize or 'see' the ways in which people's lives and experiences are transnational, mobile, and scalar. Thus, the caveat is that one cannot study transnational subjectivities or attend to multiculturalism and inequality in a transnational fashion through mobile methodologies alone. These methodologies are derived from ontological position of mobility that then informs the construction of theories and claims of knowledge we can make about the world (epistemology). Even in the context of frameworks that attend to globalization, the single most important element of such an analysis is the nation-state. Consequently, claims in relation to difference (or similarities) are based on assumptions that the nation-state and identity categories that are derived from the nation-state make sense to deploy under conditions of mobility. In other words, while there might be recognition of mobility as the defining condition of human experience in contemporary times, the frameworks and methods deployed to study the phenomenon are not founded on movement as the defining condition of humanity.

Further to this point and somewhat paradoxically, researchers do not have to move physically to gain understanding as the approaches used, such as biographies, narratives, and life stories, allow for the tracing and accounting of transnational movements. Some examples of these approaches can illustrate differences between methodologies adopted to study transnational social field versus comparative approaches which rely on static comparisons between different types of people, such as expatriates and host-country nationals; Asians and Whites; Muslim immigrants and Germans; and so forth.

In the context of organization studies and management, Calás et al. (2013) outline actions and intentions that transform entrepreneurial selves across transnational scales as the subject of research, an entrepreneur, is constantly on the move in relation to her business. By physically following the entrepreneur across geographies, nations, cities, communities, and localities, the authors outline the dynamic complexity of entrepreneurial subjectivities that arise throughout the fieldwork. Rather than adopting a priori categories that would limit the kinds of questions asked about the subject, such as through the category of female immigrant entrepreneur, the researchers start with mobility as the norm and derive observations on-the-go. Zhang and Guo (2015) provide another example that deploys mobile methodologies as they rely on in-depth interviews, observations, and textual analyses to examine the ways bilingual English/Mandarin speakers circulate in transnational social fields through linguistic, ethnic, and cultural interactions. Their methodological choice can attend to the crafting of such circulating transnational lives as the researchers recognize that their subjects actively challenge hyphenated and static identities ascribed to them in society. Similarly, Kong (2014: 273) traces the 'phenomena of creative cities and their transnational flows' by following the transnational mobilities of people, finances, discourses, technologies, and images associated with creative economies as cities compete with each other to attract talent for the purposes of economic development. Her approach is to follow these various flows through textual methods as she outlines the emergence and diffusion of creative cities as a material and discursive phenomenon.

Other research that attends to transnational social fields moves beyond interviews and texts to consider even more novel methodologies. Batnitzky et al. (2009) examine how gendered masculinities take shape among male migrant workers in London hotels and hospitals as they bring notions of gender from their homeland while interacting with 'local' notions of gender. By classifying their work as 'women's work' or 'lower-class work', male migrants produced gendered inequalities in workplaces through their transnational references and practices in relation to gender. Thus, by tracing 'gender' as their object/subject of their study inclusive of the ways it travels to new contexts, the authors provide insights about how inequalities travel and can potentially be challenged and changed once they 'arrive'.

Another example of a mobile methodology for studying transnational spaces is the work of Andrucki and Dickinson (2015) who focus on bodies and life narratives to outline new conceptualizations of centers and margins as they relate to cities and LGBT communities. By using a biographical approach and a performativity lens, the authors outline how 'axes of centrality' exist not as physical places but through the movement of bodies through different spaces and across different scales. Through the biographies of two self-identified LGBT individuals, the authors outline 'embodied conditionalities' (2015: 2) through which places become (re)imagined as central or marginal to the life experiences of LGBT people. By focusing on LGBT individuals, the scholars re-imagine the notion of core and periphery not as physical locations but, rather, as those places that become central or peripheral to the emergent life experiences, choices, and practices of communities that have long faced marginalization and discrimination. By studying mobile narratives and bodies that have to navigate different communities and cities, the researchers provide novel ways to understand transnational connections that upend existing notions of core/periphery relations. Their work provides insights as to how unexpected and unassuming cities become central to the embodied, lived experiences of LGBT subjects, and thereby create whole new narratives of what it means to be the center or the periphery.

A final example by Johnson (2013) outlines perhaps the most novel approach as she examines beauty salons as sites of production related to difference, symbolic agency, and power for Black women in the US and the historic ways different Black diasporic cultures have come to value beauty in relation to Whiteness. Using hair as text, Johnson (2013) examines how discourses and practices of beauty intersect with consumerism, agency, and empowerment for Black women through the consumption of hairstyles and products. In this example, the stories move transnationally, and are made and remade each time they are told and each time they encounter new places, people, and contexts. The movement of these stories creates transnational ties and contributes to the formation and emergence of novel subjectivities as traditional hair styles become re-interpreted. At the same time, representing both a system of representation and a culture, Black women's hair is a lens for examining the emergence of partially agentic subjectivities in US society: what are the norms and customs of Black beauty and what are the limits to natural hair in White society and organizations? Such an approach can highlight how workplace inequalities emerge when wearing one's hair naturally is a political act in the context of organizations that specifically ban particular hairstyles, such as dreadlocks and 'fros' (Johnson and Bankhead, 2014).

While each of these studies may offer a distinct angle from which we can understand and study the emergence of transnational modes, they have several commonalities. First, each provides a historic and contextual approach to the transnational perspective on the phenomenon under study. This includes focusing on people and emergent transnational subjectivities, creative cities and transnational flows, narratives on/about bodies that create alternatives transnational relations of core/periphery, and hairstyles and weaving practices. Shared between these distinct subjects/objects of study is a methodological approach that studies the lived, embodied experiences and social practices in a broader context: the interplay between the locally-grounded but transnationally informed and referent nodes that drive how the local becomes manifest are fundamental to how differences emerge, are experienced and made meaningful. Second, categories are created in precarious terms such that they guide analysis rather than dictate possibilities for understanding difference—for example, diasporic Black women's hairstyles emerge at the intersections of race, agency, and transnationally-mobile narratives of tradition and consumerism. The ways in which notions of 'diaspora', Black and belonging are held precariously as transnational achievements grounded in local practices and realities showcases the simultaneous interplay of scales. Finally, the choice of what to follow in the various studies is quite different from each other and, thus, there is not a correct or right unit, level, or scope that can be directly noted as being transnational or mobile. The relevant consideration is how the various focal points of the studies emerge through the interplay of local, national, and transnational scales and places that exist in reference to each other and emerge through referent social, epistemic, and material practices.

Despite the differences in each of the studies, the fundamental consideration around methods is guided by a broader realization and consideration of movement as the organizing and guiding ontology of the social world. Based on this, epistemological interventions are derived to examine how to create knowledge on and about a world that cannot be 'captured' or represented by the extant ideas, concepts, and theories of diversity and cross-cultural management. Consider again the example of the diasporic Black women's hairstyles—one approach that could be imagined in the diversity or cross-cultural management literature is to compare the work habits and practices of Black women, differentiated as US-born or immigrant, in the context of beauty salons. Such a comparative approach relies on making still or categorizing its subject/object of study, Black women, in order to recognize and make sense of difference. Yet under conditions of transnationalism and guided by ideas from transnational migration studies, asking the subject/object of your study to 'stay still' makes no sense. Rather, the goal is to develop and deploy mobile methodologies that can move with the subject/object of research and, in doing so, re-theorize how difference emerges across scales, places, and practices.

In all, the methodologies deployed in these and other similar transnationally-focused studies are guided by questions and concerns arriving from an ontological position of mobility and an epistemological indeterminancy where knowledge about the social world is always in a state of becoming. As new 'global assemblages' arise from the encounters of technology, people, and ideas (Ong and Collier, 2008), how we attend to these issues is a transnational realm that reflects an immediate ethical concern beyond a methodological choice. As such, mobile methodologies provide the necessary tools to uncover a world that is complex and moving, but they also necessitate reflexivity on the part of researchers to understanding for whom or what they are producing knowledge: with the arrival of the new subjects of work, how might the very concepts driving research on/about difference need to change?

Methodological and ethical considerations for MOS

In the course of this book, three main contributions of transnational migration studies have been identified and expanded on as the multiscalar global perspective, moving beyond methodological nationalism and global historical. These three analytic elements have allowed examination of new and emergent subjectivities while also contributing to an expanded and critical understanding of multiculturalism and requiring that theorizing difference take shape while cognizant of inequalities. In all, these contributions by themselves are quite relevant and potentially sufficient but additional conversation is necessary to move management and organization studies in a new direction with respect to the conceptualization and study of difference. This chapter in general and the previous sections specifically have expanded on the relevance of mobile methodologies as a new approach to the ways in which the field considers the production of knowledge and deploys methods to answer research questions. Yet beyond this, what kinds of new questions can and should management and organization scholars ask if they want to carry out research guided by transnational migration studies? And what new ethico-political epistemic considerations are there about the form of diversity and cross-cultural management research? Finally, what is the relevance of new methodologies for changing the ways research on difference, culture, and belonging takes shape?

In answering these three questions and concerns, one of the first contributions to new directions in management and organization studies can be in the form of new research questions. For example, how do transnational work practices contribute to the emergence of hybrid subjectivities as people create a sense of self that is locally-grounded but also transnationally referent? What epistemic, social, and material practices contribute to the formation of transnational human capital across different organizational contexts? Do the forms and locations of inequalities change across transnational scales in the context of multinational corporations operating in the Global South? And how might cosmopolitanism emerge as a new form of ethical behavior in professionals through their transnational movement and thereby challenge extant notions of cross-cultural 'business ethics'? What might agency look like in a transnational mode and how might it materialize (or not) differently for different people? How do new subjectivities emerge through the back and forth and back aspects of low-wage mobile workers and do/can these subjectivities challenge existing power relations in organizations/at work/in society? What conditions, narratives, and practices create a sense of transnational belonging in organizational life and how might such a sense of belonging reflect the changing form of society?

While these questions serve as exemplars of aspirational future research on difference, culture, and belonging, they all share an analytic focus on the interplay of transnational scales, inequalities, and historic context and can only be effectively examined through mobile methodologies. For the field of management and organization studies to study difference differently and in a fashion that recognizes a world on the move, then a conversation that identifies methodology as relevant but more than a choice about methods is necessary. In other words, deeper conversations around the relationship between ethics, epistemology, and research approaches must take shape in order for mobile methodologies derived from transnational migration studies to materialize.

Going back to Ahmed's (2016) contention around diversity work, why do we produce research of a particular kind in relation to difference and does our research make a difference for the organizational experiences of 'Others'? In other words, do our extant ideas about diversity and culture replicate static identity categories which then lead to decontextualized comparisons or suggestions for who or how to hire 'diverse' talent? Following from this, how do we understand the claims we make on behalf of diversity and culture when the very economic structures of neoliberalism depend on extracting labor and value from the 'Other' who is only valuable in relation to work? If we study individual experiences in organizational settings but do not acknowledge that all people have a history of coming from somewhere, what claims to knowledge can we really make? Any scholarship that aims to provide 'better' data or comparisons among different groups of people must be examined critically for the potentially dangerous forms of multiculturalism and inequality it might be perpetuating or even creating. As scholars, are we creating the concepts and organizational conditions, by way of our research findings, to extract labor from workers who have little to no choice around employment under the label of 'diversity management'?

Ultimately, the point of this book is not to offer transnational diversity or culture research but to remake the whole enterprise of research on diversity, culture, and difference in the context of management and organization studies. To this end, new directions in research cannot be contained in new methods but they must derive from ontology, epistemology, and methodology—the holy trinity of social science research. We have spent such little time understanding meta-theoretical assumptions in diversity and culture research that much of the newest advancements focus on new variable, models and modeling, or even more recently, predictive data analytics to figure out human behavior. These approaches collapse rather than acknowledge or recognize the complexity of human experiences and the fact that histories of movement impact societies in a dramatic fashion regardless of when our stories of mobility come into being.

Transnational migration studies offers insights for the ways in which societies are being remade and any claims of being native-born versus an immigrant can be debunked through examination of narratives of nationhood—when do people become citizens, when do they get to claim a place, and when do they experience professional contexts in ways that affirm their sense of being and belonging to the world? We rarely ask these kinds of questions in organizational contexts given that we use organizations as 'natural' boundaries for our scholarly examinations. Yet mobile methodologies make impossible a static, bounded unit of analysis or focus in the research project as this approach cannot allow consideration for the influence of history, context, and societal transformations on the very experiences of subjects. Moreover, scholarly work attending to difference must be able to break out of the bounded approaches that define the majority of research in management and organization studies—what difference might our work make to social justice, equality, living wages, and other important issues if we are able to study them in ways that highlight how inequalities travel via organizational practices in the context of globalized neoliberalism? And how might the value of multiculturalism be understood differently if we can examine the ways in which the language of culture sanitizes complex and contradictory aspects of lives? In all, management and organization studies can become a vanguard in examining the complexity of mobile lives and experiences across transnational scales and thereby elucidate how inequalities of various kinds materialize through organizations. Until then, we can hope to change the norms and expectations of the field with regards to the kinds of publications and research on diversity, culture, and difference that are deemed appropriate.

As a small summary, this chapter and the preceding two have laid out foundational changes to the ways in which we examine diversity, culture, and difference by:

- focusing explicitly on critiquing multiculturalism as a conformist and assimilationist approach to society;
- bringing the concept of mobile inequalities to any conversation on/ about difference given the various ways in which differences materialize and can be called on to replicate inequities transnationally; and, finally,
- by bringing mobile methodologies into the conversation at the intersections of epistemology, ethics, and methods in relation to the conceptualization and study of mobile subjects/objects.

By providing distinct frameworks, transnational migration studies has the potential to remake management and organization studies, particularly in relation to the ways scholars conceptualize and study difference.

Specifically, the field can become remade by addressing the locally-experienced yet transnationally salient aspects of professional lives. Yet more than this, a transnational and mobility derived approach to methodology means that locally-grounded experiences are contextualized in broader national and global forces. This holistic approach provides scholars an opportunity to contextualize research rather than relying on disembodied and distant categories to compare different groups of people. By examining critically power relations and hierarchies that become replicated under the notion of multiculturalism and how these become manifest in organizational life and experiences, inequalities and historic conjunctures, transnational migration studies stands to change the ways in which we examine difference. While changes to institutionalized academic norms and values generally take a long time, there is hope that with the advent of new publication forms and outlets, and increased concern around the instrumentality of research endeavors, change could happen sooner. In sum, the power of transnational migration studies is that it offers the field new concepts and approaches to study a world it recognizes as changing in a dynamic fashion. By connecting these broad changes to the ways in which we make claim on/about diversity, culture, and difference, new directions and opportunities can be carved out.

In the final chapter, future directions for research and opportunities for rethinking the foundational assumptions of the diversity and cross-cultural management field are offered. These considerations are done so with a strong emphasis on ethics and epistemology: what kinds of knowledge can we produce, and should we produce? And with what consequences? How can we hold ourselves, and the academic field, accountable for the many blind spots that have emerged with respect to missing voices, stories, and experiences in the literature focusing on diversity and culture? Finally, the last chapter offers some thoughts around what was missing in this book—those ideas that were not covered as a means to acknowledge that much more is necessary and some suggested ways to engage with topics that weren't examined in depth.

Imagining a Transnational Future for Research on Differences

What is to become of management and organization studies after an encounter with transnational migration studies? Can the field change to accommodate and offer space to theorize subjectivities that do not fit into extant categories of identity and difference as found in the diversity and cross-cultural management literatures? What possibilities are there for research in a post-multicultural and post-national world where mobility demarcates the lives, both personal and professional, of millions of people? Rather than suggest that the MOS field wholly abandon existing approaches, it is likely that the contributions from transnational migration studies, by way of this book and other interventions, will create alternatives to mainstream approaches. Change is slow in academic disciplines and in intellectual communities—often, paradigmatic fault lines emerge, demarcating and bounding particular approaches as mainstream while, at the same time, marginalizing others (Kuhn, 1962). The incommensurability discussion creeps into these decidedly political and interest-laden conversations in the sciences despite simultaneous claims that social science, much like normal science, should be infused with 'objectivity' and logical empiricism (Burrell and Morgan, 1979).

In contemporary debates among scholars in MOS, the same considerations around the 'right' and appropriate frames that should be deployed in the context of social science research still continue—an approach that is particularly relevant given that much of the research on these topics is taken up by business scholars embedded in business schools. The conservative nature of such research often contributes small, incremental knowledge rather than offering novel insights or fundamentally new theories about the nature of people, work, and organizations. Parker (2018) argues that business schools are fundamentally handmaidens of neoliberal capitalism, replicating mental models, practices, and work contexts that contribute to extractive labor and inequality. Within this context, scholars who present novel perspectives guided by different ontologies and critical epistemologies often face an uphill battle trying to publish in the most mainstream management and organization studies journal. Their work often questions the underlying tenets of the field through critical gazes and theories, such as poststructuralism, labor history, feminism and others under the broad umbrella of critical management studies (Willmott, 1992).

Yet do the performative aspects of the discipline (Fleming and Banerjee, 2016) allow us to not only change the dominant paradigms but also the context and space that determines the kinds of research considered 'valuable'? In other words, is there any opportunity to bring about change in not only the kinds of theoretical engagements that are possible in relation to the conceptualizing and study of differences but also to the very pedagogy associated with thinking about other people in the world? Can transnational migration studies change the ways in which people, work, and organizations are theorized in the context of mobility such that critical views on multiculturalism and conversations about inequality are embedded into business curriculum? The disciplines of management and organization studies have emerged throughout the decades with serious concerns around legitimacy (Alajoutsijärvi et al., 2015) in relation to 'real social science disciplines': sociology, economics and psychology. Often times, the concern over legitimacy meant that approaches that replicated the tools and approaches of aspirant-disciplines were adopted and, hence, empiricism dominated and continues to dominate research in management and organization studies.

In fact, the shift to data science in recent years has meant that many scholars are heavily reliant on quantitative and methods-driven approaches to understand the social world rather than consider the ontological and epistemological considerations guiding their research. No number of new variables, statistical models, or big data approaches can account for the human-centric complexity of a mobile world. As all the social sciences struggle to make sense of the availability of big data, AI and other advances in relation to work, management and organization studies has an opportunity to lead by re-evaluating the very paradigms guiding the majority of its research endeavors.

In the context of diversity and cross-cultural management research, the approaches and ideas available from transnational migration studies offer a set of powerful and critical frameworks that give voice and visibility to critically important issues. Yet the likelihood that existing frames guiding how scholars attend to difference are going to change rapidly is small despite growing recognition that the theories in these domains are potentially insufficient for studying a complex world. This is despite the fact that, in an ongoing fashion, scholars within the fields of diversity and cross-cultural management raise concerns about the very tools and approaches guiding difference research—a concern that dates back to the seminal article which described organizational research in a global context as a 'parochial dinosaur' (Boyacigiller and Adler, 1991). Almost three decades later, the concerns remain around the applicability of US and Western-centric theories about people, work and organizations in relation to cultural 'Others'. Little remains changed despite growing interest in diversity and cross-cultural management in academia and beyond—given the growing diversity of the workforce, the globally connected nature of organizations and economies, and the mobility of people across various boundaries, businesses of all kinds, governments, and meta-institutions have taken an interest in the consequences and impacts of a rapidly changing world.

Recently, there have been calls to change how the field of management and organization studies attends to these issues and concerns. In their recent special issue of *International Studies of Management and Organization*, the editors Guttormsen and Lauring note that several epistemologies and approaches have been silenced and/or neglected. They contend

> that the notions of silencing and neglecting are not interchangeable, but come with an important nuance. We submit that *silencing* entails the active and conscious action of marginalising particular research questions or approaches to the fringes of the intellectual field. *Neglecting*, however, is a more modest consequence of either unconscious actions by the field's elites or marginalised voices simply being overlooked on the horizon of mainstream orthodoxy. Furthermore, the two concepts are by no means typologies. Thus, gauging scholars' behaviours in isolation does not provide a fertile ground for analysis. For example, there are many CCM [cross-cultural management] researchers who are trained and sympathise with non-orthodox epistemologies and methodologies but who conduct research aligned with the expectations of the mainstream and/or external forces, in order to increase chances of publication success. (Guttormsen and Lauring, 2018: 241)

Thus, how does scholarship begin attending to those very approaches that in their current form go against mainstream orthodoxy in challenging assumptions (Özkazanç-Pan, 2015), voicing concerns related to the use of particular approaches or simply suggest that the world is too complex to be understood by the 'parochial' tools of the last century? Jonsen (2018) suggests that the tired concept of nation-state still binds many scholars in cross-cultural management, an observation that also holds true for many diversity researchers. Is it easier to abandon concepts such as identity, culture, and nation-state in totality rather than to suggest that they may be necessary but potentially insufficient to account for the lived-experiences, ideas, and practices of people who craft their lives in a transnational fashion?

Moreover, do the existing approaches we adopt and deploy by way of diversity lenses and cross-cultural management continue to replicate rather than mitigate bias, discrimination, and inequality? In his insightful recent work, Noon (2018: 198) suggests the following:

> The latest fashion of 'unconscious bias training' is a diversity intervention based on unproven suppositions and is unlikely to help eliminate racism in the workplace. Knowing about bias does not automatically result in changes in behaviour by managers and employees. Even if 'unconscious bias training' has the theoretical potential to change behaviour, it will depend on the type of racism: symbolic/modern/colour-blind, aversive or blatant. In addition, even if those deemed racist are motivated to change behaviour, structural constraints can militate against pro-diversity actions. Agency is overstated by psychology-inspired 'unconscious bias training' proponents, leading them to assume the desirability and effectiveness of this type of diversity training intervention, but from a critical diversity perspective (sociologically influenced) the training looks pointless.

As Noon notes and as is pointed out throughout this book, no amount of diversity training can overcome or begin to address mobile inequalities related to work that have taken shape over history, across transnational scales, and through various forms. Yet by changing the language and frameworks for doing and seeing diversity and cross-cultural management differently by way of transnational migration studies, a new kind of discussion might be possible.

Ethics of difference

Despite the new possibilities brought about by the mobility turn in social science, both the MOS and cross-cultural management research that attends to difference confines people to identity categories, such as gender, race, ethnicity, or culture, rather than attending to formations of self taking shape through mobility. The search for and documenting of differences in relation to values, behaviors, and experiences based on notions of self and identity derived from psychological and cultural constructs subjectifies people or makes them the subject of diversity: male/female, Black, White, Asian, culturally individualist/collectivist, bi-cultural and so forth. The documenting of differences in the context of work settings and organizations more broadly arrives out of realist ontologies that provide limited epistemic possibilities for *ways of being* and little insights into the *ways of belonging*. The performative (Butler, 1997), agentic, and reflexive dimensions of being and becoming in the context of organizational life are not sufficiently considered when a priori categorizations delimit the boundaries of the self and the kinds of meaningful practices enacted by individuals in crafting subjectivities.

In contrast, transnational migration studies provides new lenses and concepts for understanding the emergence of mobile subjectivities beyond constructivist notions of self as liminal (Beech, 2011) or in a relational fashion. The concepts available through transnational frameworks allow recognition of the new subjectivities that result from encounters between and among people in the context of history, power relations, economic structures, political discourses, and socio-cultural practices taking shape in society. Transnational modes of analysis uncover that, while people may 'assimilate' on their own terms and in their own ways, they may, at the same time, stay connected to other places, spaces, and people through intention and action in transnational social fields. Such an analytic position recognizes that normalized ways of differentiating between and among people in one scale need to be held precariously given that they may not have epistemic equivalents in other places and spaces.

Yet more than a discussion on/about epistemology in relation to research, the search for difference also requires a conversation around ethics: what are the ethico-political considerations of searching for and documenting differences in the context of organizations? How do our research endeavors replicate business interests given the increasing profitability and interest in 'managing diversity' and the assumed competitive advantages brought about by difference (Cox and Blake, 1991; Lynch, 2017)? In other words, are the axioms of difference becoming co-opted by organizations operating under conditions of globalized neoliberalism such that difference becomes a scalpel to extract labor precisely rather than a way to recognize the value and dignity of each worker? Doing diversity and cross-cultural management research is also doing ethics of a particular kind: whose voices, bodies, and ideas are deemed valuable for the purposes of work and organizations and whose do we try to assimilate through 'diversity training' or 'cultural sensitivity'? And in doing so, who benefits? Without asking these questions, any new paradigm will yield powerful insights but, in a fashion, those insights will be decoupled from an ethical consideration around the consequences of our collective knowledge production on/about difference. Transnational migration studies not only provides novel language and concepts in relation to studying the new social, cultural, and political transformation of our time, but it does so with a particular sensitivity toward historical conjunctures and inequality. At this moment in human history, which trajectories will allow us to create a just and equal world of work?

New directions

In summary, transmigrant, hybrid, and cosmopolitan subjectivities as new lenses each offer innovative directions in studying and understanding people and difference in the context of work and organizations. Transmigrants focuses on the crafting of agentic, reflexive subjectivities in a multiscalar fashion while hybrid selves refers to the formations of selves that emerge through novel combinations of existing discourses, socio-cultural and material practices. Finally, cosmopolitans focuses on those people who craft an orientation to the world on the go as they engage in work opportunities across different contexts. Cosmopolitanism opens us possibilities for rethinking how people 'do work' under conditions of mobility and in relation to being an anchored yet pivoting 'citizen of world'. In all, these different subjectivities provide much needed theoretical nuance and complexity to the kinds of selves taking shape in today's dynamic societies.

In addition, transnational migration studies provide novel contributions for rethinking some of the fundamental ideas of diversity and cross-cultural management. Rather than accepting multiculturalism as a positive element of changing societies, the critical consideration is around the ways in which delimited identity categories offer little choice in reflecting one's transgressions across boundaries. In fact, multiculturalism can only partially theorize transnational lives at the moment of encounter—the ways in which people create meaning and engage in narratives and practices that go beyond any one nation-state are simply invisible to multiculturalism's epistemological framework. Transnational lives simply do not translate fully to the categories available for them under conditions of multiculturalism. Consequently, mobile subjectivities provide an alternative not only to theorizing individuals but also to our rethinking about the limits of multiculturalism.

Another contribution from transnational migration studies is to the theorization and consideration of inequality. Much of diversity and cross-cultural management research does not attend to inequality despite theorizing near it through the language of perceived fairness/unfairness. Yet much more is necessary in order to move beyond difference as a marker of individuals to how the ways in which difference is theorized and studied in the context of work are embedded in neoliberal contexts. Without acknowledging the historic context of differences and their contemporary manifestation in relation to inequality today, researchers are not able to fully present the dark side of diversity. Mobile inequalities speak to these issues in relation to movement: how do new regimes of inequality emerge through worker mobility and with what consequence? By addressing the ways in which inequalities emerge and move, scholars of diversity and cross-cultural management can begin to understand the experiences of individuals in a complex fashion.

Finally, transnational migration studies offer insights about the ways in which methodologies have to be reconsidered in order to attend to people, ideas, and practices on the move. Rather than novel methods, the consideration is equally on the theory of methods and the approaches deployed. The examples presented in this book derive their novelty from research questions that are guided by a mobility lens and, in doing so, investigate the ways in which different subjects/objects of research move through history, space, and place. Each of the research projects provides novel ways to understand the complexity of transnationalism as a mode of life and experience. In all, they present nuanced ways of being and belonging across a variety of examples and transnational scales.

In all, transnational migration studies offer conceptually distinct frameworks to study the intersections of people, difference, and organizations inclusive of new research questions derived through a transnational lens. Table 2 summarizes key points of difference between extant diversity and cross-cultural research focused on people and difference, and the possibilities for selves and research arriving out of transnational migration frameworks.

Fundamentally, transnational modes of thinking and analyzing allow us to consider the composition and coming together of society rather than a reflection of the boundaries/boundedness of nation-states. They provide insights as to what citizenship means beyond an accident of birth and turn our gaze to the ways in which historical conjunctures impact contemporary economic arrangements, political debates and cultural institutions. For organization scholars who want to study diversity and

Table 2: Guiding assumptions of research attending to difference

	Mainstream diversity	Cross-cultural/International management	Transnational migration studies
Ontologies	Realist: differences are real in ontological terms and researchers can aim to represent them accurately through constructs	Realist: differences are real in ontological terms and researchers can aim to represent them accurately through constructs and theories	Mobility: ontology that recognizes world on-the-move
	Relational: differences arise from relational exchanges between people	Realist/Objectivist: Social world out there and theories inclusive of frameworks can be used to study differences	Difference takes shape through encounters in a world that is constantly in a state of becoming
	Frameworks can be used to capture differences	Difference is rooted in realist/objectivist ideologies: they are out there for researchers to represent	Social world marked by movement and various migrations whose ontological status is indeterminable and constantly moving
Notion of self	Psychological constructs, such as schemas, to reflect bounded, rational self	Cultural schemas to conceptualize and differentiate people; culture as set of values, attitudes, behaviors unique to nations and groups of people	Mobile subjectivities taking shape across multiple scales of reference: precarious and fluid
	Identity as reflection of self, use of psychological constructs to 'get at' values, attitudes, motivations of people to differentiate between them; identity formation as relational	Cultures are stable over time such that change is small and incremental	Historically formed and reformed in contemporary contexts
	Diversity reflects differences across gender, race, ethnicity, class, etc.	Culture makes a difference in relation to how people work and management and how they might need to be managed	Simultaneously anchored and pivoting in transnational social fields
		Bi-cultural or multicultural people identify with more than culture	Embedded in multiscalar transnational social fields, historically contextualized, economic dispossession can be marker of their social experiences and everyday lives
		Expatriates, host-country nationals, home-country nationals, native, local, foreigner	Transmigrants, hybrids, cosmopolitans, nomads

(continued)

	Mainstream diversity	Cross-cultural/International management	Transnational migration studies
Nation and society	Defined by political and geographic borders Citizenship as belonging to a specific nation Coming together of different people, nation as container for people and society If migration acknowledged, attended to through category of immigrant	Defined by political and geographic borders; movement acknowledged through immigration Cultural values can be studied at level of nation: nations have unique and different cultures that can be used to study its society and citizens Citizenship as political belonging: having passport of a particular nation	Historically constituted through discourses, practices, and ideologies of particular groups; nations no longer equated with political form of society or ethos of only one group Questions location and nature of society in relation to the nation-state Migration defining condition of human experience and societies globally; structuring of inequalities key concern
Epistemology and research questions	Conducts research relevant for diversity management Examines relationship between diversity and individual, team and organizational level measures/outcomes *Research questions:* What are best practices for recruiting women to senior leadership positions? Are there differences between minority and White employees in turnover intentions? What are psychological antecedents of positive group dynamics in multicultural teams?	Cultural values used to differentiate between people in different contexts Culture makes a difference in work values and how people might need to be managed *Research questions:* What are reliable measures of effectiveness in expatriate cross-cultural training? How does managerial cognition develop in multicultural individuals? What are the challenges of transferring HR practices from high power distance HQs to subsidiaries in low power distance nations?	Epistemic claims are always in state of becoming vs finality Understand *ways of being* and *ways of belonging* in multiscalar fashion; uncover transnational forms *Research questions:* How do transnational knowledge workers enact 'identity' belongings'? (Colic-Peisker, 2010) How do mobile bodies reconfigure core/periphery notions? (Andrucki and Dickinson, 2015) How do international professionals 'regulate their exposure' to the locals and localities? (Nowicka and Kaweh, 2009)

(continued)

Table 2: Guiding assumptions of research attending to difference (continued)

	Mainstream diversity	Cross-cultural/International management	Transnational migration studies
Favored methodologies	Mix of qualitative and quantitative approaches; positive and some critical approaches	Positivist approaches to capture differences based on culture: values, attitudes, behaviors, practices, and so on	Mobile methodologies, such as life stories, shadowing, biographies, tracing of phenomena, reading of 'texts' (such as hair as text), researcher moves with the subject/object of research; may be physical, virtual, text, or social media based, material, discursive, embodied
	Interviews, observations, fieldwork; can include text and discourse analysis	Interviews, observations, fieldwork	
	Categories (gender, race, ethnicity, education) often used as variables to compare/contrast individuals and groups across dimensions	Survey instruments to measure cultural differences	Derived from research questions attending to inequalities, historic conjunctures and different interrelated scales (local to global)

attend to difference, transnational modes provide insights as to new ways of understanding people in the form of mobile subjectivities and move us to consider the question of who/what is the subject of diversity research. By relying on new ontologies and epistemologies available from a transnational migration studies framework, we can offer insights about how the social world is being made and remade and the consequences of such action and intention for the (organizational) lives of people around the world.

One of the main ways that research attending to differences can be done in a manner derived from transnational migration studies is to acknowledge the ways in which historic mobility matters to contemporary experiences at work and in organizations broadly. For studying difference in a manner that is derived from transnational migration studies, one should ask research questions that can address or at least acknowledge the role of historic movement. But more than this, research must also attend to the back and forth dimensions of experiences. History is not only about what took shape in the past but is also a way to acknowledge the ways people, ideas, and practices cross borders of various kinds on an ongoing basis. History is always in the making and, consequently, static approaches to difference that aim to categorize people will not be able to 'see' or study the ongoing, relational, and transnational dimensions of subjectivities in relation to epistemic, social, and material aspects.

Further, any new approach must be done so with the understanding that diversity and cross-cultural management research in the context of management and organization studies has been guided by dominant empiricist and positivist paradigms for decades. Any change will not only require new theories and framework, but also new approaches to teaching difference, a pedagogical intervention—while not the focus of this book, teaching and research often go hand in hand such that research informs many of the concepts and practices we infuse in our language and curriculum. Is there hope for changing the ways we experience work and organizations if we intervene in the ways difference, diversity, and culture are taught? A critical perspective is vital to contextualizing and providing conversations around the many inequities facing people due to organizational practices in the context of changing societies. It is imperative for scholars to contextualize the ways societies are changing and whether our approaches can represent the myriad of experiences, subjectivities, and changing nature, location, and form of society. What does citizenship look like under conditions of transnational mobility, and can the categories of diversity and cross-cultural management accommodate them? Race, ethnicity, and culture have now become contested domains rather than simple reflections of identity or nation-states. The ways in which people live their personal and professional lives, and the various practices that allow them to create a sense of being and a sense of belonging to the social world must be acknowledged in any conversation about difference.

Scholars of diversity and cross-cultural management must now take the time to realize the shortcomings of existing theories and approaches, and consider how mobility impacts the ways work and lives are organized. Organizations provide opportunities for people to encounter differences—yet how we frame these differences and attempt to erase or amplify them is something that has yet to be examined critically. In going back to Ahmed's (2016) discussion around diversity work: when will we no longer need to do this kind of work, and how might acknowledging changing societal norms and values contribute to its undoing? As far-right sentiment and neo-nationalism grows, so do resistances and challenges to their guiding narratives of 'racial/ethnic purity', separation of people, and hatred and fear of 'outsiders'. Many societies are now at an inflection point in relation to the future of democracies, free movement of people, and ethics in a world filled with contested claims, authoritarianism, and mounting inequalities and incivilities. In the darkest hours of humanity, acknowledging our collective mobile history throughout eons debunks any notion of boundaries—those man-made lines that have, century after century, attempted to create social and cultural differences between people as natural rather than fictional in an attempt to rule, dominate, or obliterate.

What if these approaches were no longer the norm in social science research but, instead, new ways of seeing people and their complex lives offered us the opportunity to create collective futures based on justice, equity, and inclusion? The urgency for scholarship that can attend to and challenge 'alternative facts' about issues relevant for women, minorities, immigrants, and climate change among others has never been greater in recent years. It is with hope and trepidation that I suggest transnational perspectives may debunk fundamentalist, extremist, and polarizing discourses that are reshaping societies as these frameworks require us to face the present by acknowledging shared histories and migratory experiences. In such a world, what are the possibilities and responsibilities of diversity and cross-cultural management scholarship after migration?

References

AACSB (The Association to Advance Collegiate Schools of Business) (2018) '2013 Eligibility and procedures and accreditation standards for business school accreditation', last revised July 1, 2018, www.aacsb.edu/-/ media/aacsb/docs/accreditation/business/standards-and-tables/2018-business-standards.ashx?la=en

Adam Cobb, J. (2016) 'How firms shape income inequality: Stakeholder power, executive decision making, and the structuring of employment relationships', *Academy of Management Review*, 41(2): 324–48.

Adler, N.J. (1983) 'Organizational development in a multicultural environment', *The Journal of Applied Behavioral Science*, 19(3): 349–65.

Ahmed, S. (2007a) '"You end up doing the document rather than doing the doing": Diversity, race equality and the politics of documentation', *Ethnic and Racial Studies*, 30(4): 590–609.

Ahmed, S. (2007b) 'The language of diversity', *Ethnic and Racial Studies*, 30(2): 235–56.

Ahmed, S. (2016) 'Diversity work', https://feministkilljoys. com/2016/07/12/evidence/

Ahonen, P. and Tienari, J. (2015) 'Ethico-politics of diversity and its production', in A. Pullen and C. Rhodes (eds), *The Routledge Companion to Ethics, Politics and Organizations*, Routledge, pp 271–86.

Alajoutsijärvi, K., Juusola, K. and Siltaoja, M. (2015) 'The legitimacy paradox of business schools: Losing by gaining?', *Academy of Management Learning & Education*, 14(2): 277–91.

Alba, R. and Nee, V. (2009) *Remaking the American Mainstream: Assimilation and Contemporary Immigration*, Cambridge, MA: Harvard University Press.

Albrecht, M.H. (ed) (2001) *International HRM: Managing Diversity in the Workplace*, Malden, MA: Blackwell Publishing.

Alt, J. and Iversen, T. (2017). 'Inequality, labor market segmentation, and preferences for redistribution', *American Journal of Political Science*, 61(1): 21–36.

Amelina, A., Nergiz, D.D., Faist, T. and Glick Schiller, N. (2012) *Beyond Methodological Nationalism: Research Methodologies for Cross-border Studies*, New York: Routledge.

Anderson, B. (1983/2006) *Imagined Communities: Reflections on the Origin and Spread of Nationalism*, London: Verso Books.

Andrevski, G., Richard, O.C., Shaw, J.D. and Ferrier, W.J. (2014) 'Racial diversity and firm performance: the mediating role of competitive intensity', *Journal of Management*, 40(3): 820–44.

Andrucki, M.J. and Dickinson, J. (2015) 'Rethinking centers and margins in geography: Bodies, life course, and the performance of transnational space', *Annals of the Association of American Geographers*, 105(1): 203–18.

Anzaldúa, G. (1987) *Borderlands: La Frontera* (Vol. 3), San Francisco: Aunt Lute.

Appadurai, A. (1996) *Modernity at Large: Cultural Dimensions of Globalization* (Vol. 1), University of Minnesota Press.

Appiah, K.A. (2010) *Cosmopolitanism: Ethics in a World of Strangers (Issues of our Time)*, WW Norton and Company.

Arango, J. and Baldwin-Edwards, M. (2014) *Immigrants and the Informal Economy in Southern Europe*, New York: Routledge.

Archer, M.S. (2007) 'The ontological status of subjectivity: The missing link between structure and agency', in C. Lawson, J. Latsis, and N. Martins (eds), *Contributions to Social Ontology, Routledge Series on Critical Realism 15*, New York: Routledge, pp 17–31.

Argun, B.E. (2017) *Turkey in Germany: The Transitional Sphere of Deutschkei*, New York: Routledge.

Asher, N. (2008) 'Listening to hyphenated Americans: Hybrid identities of youth from immigrant families', *Theory Into Practice*, 47(1): 12–19.

Atewologun, D., Sealy, R. and Vinnicombe, S. (2015) 'Revealing intersectional dynamics in organizations: Introducing "intersectional identity work"', *Gender, Work and Organization*, 23(3), DOI: 10.1111/gwao.12082

Auer, D., Bonoli, G., Fossati, F., and Liechti, F. (2016) 'The matching hierarchies model: Evidence from a survey experiment on employers' hiring intent of immigrant applicants', https://papers.ssrn.com/sol3/papers.cfm?abstract_id=2750794

Bakhtin, M.M. (1977) 'The problem of the text (an essay in philosophical analysis),' *Soviet Studies in Literature*, 14(1): 3–33.

Bakhtin, M.M. (1981) *The Dialogic Imagination: Four Essays* (Vol. 1). Trans. by Caryl Emerson and Michael Holquist, Austin, TX: University of Texas Press.

Banerjee-Guha, S. (ed) (2010) *Accumulation by Dispossession: Transformative Cities in the New Global Order*, New Delhi: Sage Publications India.

Baron, J.N. and Bielby, W.T. (1980) 'Bringing the firms back in: Stratification, segmentation, and the organization of work,' *American Sociological Review*, 45(5) 737–65.

Barrientos, S., Gereffi, G. and Rossi, A. (2011) 'Economic and social upgrading in global production networks: A new paradigm for a changing world', *International Labour Review*, 150(3–4): 319–40.

Baruch, Y., Altman, Y. and Tung, R.L. (2016) 'Career mobility in a global era: Advances in managing expatriation and repatriation', *Academy of Management Annals*, 10(1): 841–89.

Basch, L., Glick Schiller, N. and Blanc, C.S. (eds) (1994) *Nations Unbound: Transnational Projects, Postcolonial Predicaments, and Deterritorialized Nation-States*, New York: Routledge.

Batnitzky, A., McDowell, L. and Dyer, S. (2009) 'Flexible and strategic masculinities: The working lives and gendered identities of male migrants in London', *Journal of Ethnic and Migration Studies*, 35(8): 1275–93.

Baubock, R. and Faist, T. (eds) (2010) *Diaspora and Transnationalism: Concepts, Theories and Methods*, Amsterdam, Netherlands: Amsterdam University Press.

Beech, N. (2011) 'Liminality and the practices of identity reconstruction', *Human Relations*, 64(2): 285–302.

Bell, E.L.E. (1990) 'The bicultural life experience of career-oriented black women', *Journal of Organizational Behavior*, 11(6): 459–77.

Bell, M.P., Kwesiga, E.N. and Berry, D.P. (2010) 'Immigrants: The new "invisible men and women" in diversity research', *Journal of Managerial Psychology*, 25(2): 177–88.

Bell, M.P., Marquardt, D. and Berry, D.P. (2014) '"Diversity," immigration, and the new American multi-racial hierarchy', *Journal of Managerial Psychology*, 29(3): 285–303.

Bendl, R., Bleijenbergh, I., Henttonen, E. and Mills, A.J. (eds) (2015) *The Oxford Handbook of Diversity in Organizations*, Oxford: Oxford University Press.

Bendl, R., Fleischmann, A., and Hofmann, R. (2009) 'Queer theory and diversity management: Reading codes of conduct from a queer perspective', *Journal of Management and Organization*, 15(05): 625–38.

Bendl, R., Fleischmann, A. and Walenta, C. (2008) 'Diversity management discourse meets queer theory', *Gender in Management*, 23(6): 382–94.

Benhabib, S. (2002) *The Claims of Culture: Equality and Diversity in the Global Era*, Princeton, NJ: Princeton University Press.

Benhabib, S. (2004) *The Rights of Others: Aliens, Residents, and Citizens* (Vol. 5), Cambridge: Cambridge University Press.

Benhabib, S. (2008) *Another Cosmopolitanism*, Oxford: Oxford University Press.

Benschop, Y. and Verloo, M. (2006) 'Sisyphus' sisters: can gender mainstreaming escape the genderedness of organizations?', *Journal of Gender Studies*, 15(1): 19–33.

Benschop, Y., Holgersson, C., Van den Brink, M. and Wahl, A. (2015) 'Future challenges for practices of diversity management in organizations', in *The Oxford Handbook for Diversity in Organizations*, Oxford: Oxford University Press, 553–74.

Bernstein, M. and De la Cruz, M. (2009) '"What are you?": Explaining identity as a goal of the multiracial Hapa movement', *Social Problems*, 56(4): 722–45.

Berrey, E. (2014) 'Breaking glass ceilings, ignoring dirty floors: The culture and class bias of diversity management', *American Behavioral Scientist*, 58(2): 347–70.

Berry, D. and Bell, M.P. (2012) 'Inequality in organizations: Stereotyping, discrimination, and labor law exclusions', *Equality, Diversity and Inclusion: An International Journal*, 31(3): 236–48.

Berger, L.J., Essers, C. and Himi, A. (2017) 'Muslim employees within 'white' organizations: The case of Moroccan workers in the Netherlands', *The International Journal of Human Resource Management*, 28(8): 1119–39.

Beugelsdijk, S., Kostova, T. and Roth, K. (2017) 'An overview of Hofstede-inspired country-level culture research in international business since 2006', *Journal of International Business Studies*, 48(1): 30–47.

Bhabha, H.K. (ed) (1990) *Nation and Narration*, New York: Routledge.

Bhatia, S. (2012) 'Acculturation and the dialogical formation of immigrant identity: Race and culture in diaspora spaces', in H.J.M. Herman and T. Gieser, T. (eds), *Handbook of Dialogical Self Theory*, Cambridge: Cambridge University Press, pp 115–31.

Bhatia, S. and Ram, A. (2001) 'Rethinking "acculturation" in relation to diasporic cultures and postcolonial identities', *Human Development*, 44(1): 1–18.

Bhatia, S. and Ram, A. (2009) 'Theorizing identity in transnational and diaspora cultures: A critical approach to acculturation', *International Journal of Intercultural Relations*, 33(2): 140–49.

Biemann, T. and Andresen, M. (2010) 'Self-initiated foreign expatriates versus assigned expatriates: two distinct types of international careers?', *Journal of Managerial Psychology*, 25(4): 430–48.

Björkman, I. and Lervik, J.E. (2007) 'Transferring HR practices within multinational corporations', *Human Resource Management Journal*, 17(4): 320–35.

Bleijenbergh, I. and Fielden, S.L. (2015) 'Examining diversity in organizations from critical perspectives', in R. Bendl, I. Bleijenbergh, E. Henttonen (eds), *The Oxford Handbook of Diversity in Organizations*, Oxford: Oxford University Press, pp. 539–52.

Blunt, A. (2007) 'Cultural geographies of migration: Mobility, transnationality and diaspora', *Progress in Human Geography*, 31(5): 684–94.

Boccagni, P. (2012) 'Even a transnational social field must have its boundaries: Methodological options, potentials and dilemmas for researching transnationalism,' in C. Vargas-Silva (ed), *Handbook of Research Methods in Migration*, Northampton, MA: Edward Elgar, pp 295–318.

Bonilla-Silva, E. (2006) *Racism with Racists*, Lanham, MD: Rowman and Littlefield.

Boxenbaum, E. (2006) 'Lost in translation: The making of Danish diversity management', *American Behavioral Scientist*, 49(7): 939–48.

Boyacigiller, N.A. and Adler, N.J. (1991) 'The parochial dinosaur: Organizational science in a global context', *Academy of Management Review*, 16(2): 262–90.

Brah, A. (2005) *Cartographies of Diaspora: Contesting Identities*, New York: Routledge.

Brah, A. and Phoenix, A. (2004) 'Ain't I a woman? Revisiting intersectionality', *Journal of International Women's Studies*, 5(3): 75–86.

Brannen, M.Y. and Thomas, D.C. (2010) 'Bicultural individuals in organizations: Implications and opportunity', *International Journal of Cross-Cultural Management*, 10(1): 5–16.

Brewster, C., Harris, H. and Petrovic, J. (2001) 'Globally mobile employees: Managing the mix', *Journal of Professional HRM*, 25: 11–15.

Brewster, C., Sparrow, P. and Harris, H. (2005) 'Towards a new model of globalizing HRM', *The International Journal of Human Resource Management Group*, 16(6): 949–70.

Brubaker, R. (2013) 'Categories of analysis and categories of practice: A note on the study of Muslims in European countries of immigration', *Ethnic and Racial Studies*, 36(1): 1–8.

Burrell, G. and Morgan, G. (1979) *Sociological Paradigms and Organisational Analysis*, Farnham: Ashgate Publishing.

Butcher, M. (2009) 'Ties that bind: The strategic use of transnational relationships in demarcating identity and managing difference', *Journal of Ethnic and Migration Studies*, 35(8): 1353–71.

Butler, J. (1997) *Excitable Speech: A Politics of the Performative*, New York, NY: Psychology Press.

Butler, J. and Athanasiou, A. (2013) *Dispossession: The Performative in the Political*, Malden, MA: Polity Press.

Caglar, A., and Glick Schiller, N. (2015) 'A multiscalar perspective on cities and migration. A comment on the symposium', *Sociologica*, 9(2): DOI: 10.2383/81432

Calás, M.B., Holgersson, C. and Smircich, L. (2009) '"Diversity Management"? Translation? Travel?', *Scandinavian Journal of Management*, 25(4): 349–51.

Calás, M.B., Ou, H. and Smircich, L. (2013) '"Woman" on the move: mobile subjectivities after intersectionality', *Equality, Diversity and Inclusion: An International Journal*, 32(8): 708–31.

Calás, M.B. and Smircich, L. (1999) 'Past postmodernism? Reflections and tentative directions', *Academy of Management Review*, 24(4): 649–72.

Calás, M.B. and Smircich, L. (2011) 'In the back and forth of transmigration: Thinking organization studies in a transnational key', in E.L. Jeanes, D. Knights and P.Y Martin (eds), *Handbook of Gender, Work and Organization*, West Sussex: John Wiley and Sons, pp 411–28.

Calás, M.B. and Smircich, L. (2018) 'Opening spaces and living in the limits: Attempts at intervening in organization studies', in Debra A. Noumair and Abraham B. Shani (eds) *Research in Organizational Change and Development*, ebook series, Emerald Publishing, pp 389–420.

Calás, M.B., Smircich, L., Tienari, J. and Ellehave, C.F. (2010) 'Editorial: Observing globalized capitalism: Gender and ethnicity as an entry point', *Gender, Work and Organization*, 17(3): 243–47.

Campbell, K. and Mínguez-Vera, A. (2008) 'Gender diversity in the boardroom and firm financial performance', *Journal of Business Ethics*, 83(3): 435–51.

Canclini, N.G. (1995) *Hybrid Cultures: Strategies for Entering and Leaving Modernity*, Minneapolis, MN: University of Minnesota Press.

Capetillo-Ponce, J. and Kretsedemas, P. (2013) 'Introduction: The problem of migrant marginality', in P. Kretsedemas, J. Capetillo-Ponce and G. Jacobs (eds) *Migrant Marginality: A Transnational Perspective*, New York: Routledge, pp 1–24.

Castilla, E.J. (2008) 'Gender, race, and meritocracy in organizational careers 1', *American Journal of Sociology*, 113(6): 1479–526.

Castles, S. (2012) 'Understanding the relationship between methodology and methods', in C. Vargas-Silva (ed), *Handbook of Research Methods in Migration*, Northampton, MA: Edward Elgar, pp 7–25.

Castles, S., De Haas, H. and Miller, M.J. (2013) *The Age of Migration: International Population Movements in the Modern World* (5th edn), New York: Palgrave Macmillan.

Chao, M.M., Takeuchi, R. and Farh, J.L. (2017) 'Enhancing cultural intelligence: The roles of implicit culture beliefs and adjustment', *Personnel Psychology*, 70(1): 257–92.

Chatman, J.A. (2010) 'Norms in mixed sex and mixed race work groups', *Academy of Management Annals*, 4(1): 447–84.

Chatman, J.A. and Flynn, F.J. (2001) 'The influence of demographic heterogeneity on the emergence and consequences of cooperative norms in work teams', *Academy of Management Journal*, 44(5): 956–74.

Chatterjee, P. (2004) *The Politics of the Governed*, Columbia, NY: Columbia University Press.

Chernilo, D. (2006) 'Social theory's methodological nationalism myth and reality', *European Journal of Social Theory*, 9(1): 5–22.

Colic-Peisker, V. (2010) 'Free floating in the cosmopolis? Exploring the identity-belonging of transnational knowledge workers', *Global Networks*, 10(4): 467–88.

Collins, P.H. (1998) 'It's all in the family: Intersections of gender, race, and nation', *Hypatia*, 13(3), 62–82.

Colquitt, J.A. and Rodell, J.B. (2015) 'Measuring justice and fairness', in R.S. Cropanzano and M.L. Ambrose (ed), *Oxford Handbook of Justice in the Workplace*, Oxford: Oxford University Press, pp 187–204.

Conboy, K. and Kelly, C. (2016) 'What evidence is there that mentoring works to retain and promote employees, especially diverse employees, within a single company?', Cornell University, ILR School, http://digitalcommons.ilr.cornell.edu/student/116/

Coombes, A.E. and Brah, V. (2000) 'Introduction: The conundrum of mixing', in A. Brah and A.E. Coombes (eds), *Hybridity and its Discontents: Politics, Science, Culture*, New York: Routledge, pp 1–16.

Cox, T.H. and Blake, S. (1991) 'Managing cultural diversity: Implications for organizational competitiveness', *The Executive*, 5(3) 45–56.

Creese, G. and Wiebe, B. (2012) '"Survival employment": Gender and deskilling among African immigrants in Canada', *International Migration*, 50(5): 56–76.

Crenshaw, K. (1991) 'Mapping the margins: Intersectionality, identity politics, and violence against women of color', *Stanford Law Review*, 43(6): 1241–99.

Crul, M. (2016) 'Super-diversity vs. assimilation: How complex diversity in majority–minority cities challenges the assumptions of assimilation', *Journal of Ethnic and Migration Studies*, 42(1): 54–68.

D'Andrea, A. (2006) 'Neo-nomadism: A theory of post-identitarian mobility in the global age', *Mobilities*, 1(1): 95–119.

Daniel, G.R. (2018) *Degrees of Mixture, Degrees of Freedom: Genomics, Multiculturalism, and Race in Latin America*, Durham, NC: Duke University Press.

Datta, A. (2009) 'Places of everyday cosmopolitanisms: East European construction workers in London', *Environment and Planning A*, 41(2): 353–70.

Davis, K. (2008) 'Intersectionality as buzzword: A sociology of science perspective on what makes a feminist theory successful', *Feminist Theory*, 9(1): 67–85.

De Haas, H. (2005) 'International migration, remittances and development: myths and facts', *Third World Quarterly*, 26(8): 1269–84.

DiTomaso, N., Post, C. and Parks-Yancy, R. (2007) 'Workforce diversity and inequality: Power, status, and numbers', *Annual Review of Sociology*, 33: 473–501.

Djelic, M. and Quack, S. (eds) (2010) *Transnational Communities: Shaping Global Economic Governance*, Cambridge: Cambridge University Press.

DuBois, W.E.B. (1903/1965) *The Souls of Black Folk*, London: Longmans, Green and Co.

DuBois, W.E.B. (1940/2012) *Dusk of Dawn*, New Brunswick, NJ: Transaction Publishers.

Durr, E. (2011) 'To Belong in Aotearoa New Zealand: Latin American migrant experiences in multicultural Auckland', *Journal of Ethnic and Migration Studies*, 37(3): 503–19.

Dwyer, C. (2000) 'Negotiating diasporic identities: Young British South Asian Muslim women', *Women's Studies International Forum*, 23(4): 475–86.

Eagly, A.H. and Chin, J.L. (2010) 'Diversity and leadership in a changing world', *American Psychologist*, 65(3): 216–24.

Edwards, T., Sánchez-Mangas, R., Jalette, P., Lavelle, J. and Minbaeva, D. (2016) 'Global standardization or national differentiation of HRM practices in multinational companies? A comparison of multinationals in five countries', *Journal of International Business Studies*, 47(8): 997–1021.

Ehrkamp, P. (2005) 'Placing identities: Transnational practices and local attachments of Turkish immigrants in Germany', *Journal of Ethnic and Migration Studies*, 31(2): 345–64.

Ehrkamp, P. (2016) 'Beyond the mosque: Turkish immigrants and the practice and politics of Islam in Duisburg-Marxloh, Germany', in P. Hopkins (ed), *Geographies of Muslim Identities*, New York: Routledge, pp 21–38.

Ehrkamp, P. and Leitner, H. (2006) 'Rethinking immigration and citizenship: new spaces of migrant transnationalism and belonging', *Environment and Planning*, 38: 1591–97.

Ely, R.J. and Thomas, D.A. (2001) 'Cultural diversity at work: The effects of diversity perspectives on work group processes and outcomes', *Administrative Science Quarterly*, 46(2): 229–73.

Ensher, E.A. and Murphy, S.E. (1997) 'Effects of race, gender, perceived similarity, and contact on mentor relationships', *Journal of Vocational Behavior*, 50(3): 460–81.

Erdal, M.B. and Oeppen, C. (2013) 'Migrant balancing acts: Understanding the interactions between integration and transnationalism', *Journal of Ethnic and Migration Studies*, 39(6): 867–84.

Faist, T. (2010) 'Towards transnational studies: World theories, transnationalisation and changing institutions', *Journal of Ethnic and Migration Studies*, 36(10): 1665–87.

Faist, T. (2013) 'The mobility turn: A new paradigm for the social sciences?', *Ethnic and Racial Studies*, 36(11): 1637–46.

Fanon, F. (1952/2008) *Black Skin, White Masks*, New York: Grove Press.

Fanon, F. (1963) *The Wretched of the Earth*, New York: Grove/Atlantic, Inc.

Faria, A. (2015) 'Reframing diversity management', in R. Bendl, I. Bleijenbergh, E. Henttonen, and A.J. Mills (eds), *The Oxford Handbook of Diversity in Organizations*, Oxford: Oxford University Press, pp 127–52.

Ferner, A., Almond, P. and Colling, T. (2005) 'Institutional theory and the cross-national transfer of employment policy: The case of "workforce diversity" in US multinationals', *Journal of International Business Studies*, 36(3): 304–21.

Fiske, S.T. and Taylor, S.E. (2013) *Social Cognition: From Brains to Culture*, Thousand Oaks, CA: Sage.

Fitzgerald, J. (2007) *Big White Lie: Chinese Australians in White Australia*, Sydney: UNSW Press.

Fitzsimmons, S.R. (2013) 'Multicultural employees: A framework for understanding how they contribute to organizations', *Academy of Management Review*, 38(4): 525–49.

Fleming, P. and Banerjee, S.B. (2016) 'When performativity fails: Implications for critical management studies', *Human Relations*, 69(2): 257–76.

Frenkel, M. and Shenhav, Y. (2006) 'From binarism back to hybridity: A postcolonial reading of management and organization studies', *Organization Studies*, 27(6): 855–76.

Garrido, M.R. and Codó, E. (2017) 'Deskilling and delanguaging African migrants in Barcelona: Pathways of labour market incorporation and the value of "global" English', *Globalisation, Societies and Education*, 15(1): 29–49.

Ghorashi, H. and Ponzoni, E. (2014) 'Reviving agency: Taking time and making space for rethinking diversity and inclusion', *European Journal of Social Work*, 17(2): 161–74.

Gibson-Graham, J.K. (1997) 'The end of capitalism (as we knew it): A feminist critique of political economy', *Capital and Class*, 21(2): 186–88.

Gilroy, P. (1993) *The Black Atlantic*, Cambridge, MA: Harvard University Press.

Glick Schiller, N. (1999) 'Transmigrants and nation-states: Something old and something new in U.S. immigrant experience', in C. Hirschman, J. DeWind, and P. Kasinitz (eds), *Handbook of International Migration*, Thousand Oaks, CA: Sage, pp 94–119.

Glick Schiller, N. (2010) 'A global perspective on transnational migration: Theorizing migration without methodological nationalism', in R. Bauböck, and T. Faist (eds), *Diaspora and Transnationalism: Concepts, Theories and Methods*, Amsterdam: Amsterdam University Press, pp 109–29.

Glick Schiller, N. (2015) 'Explanatory frameworks in transnational migration studies: the missing multi-scalar global perspective', *Ethnic and Racial Studies*, 38(13): 2275–82.

Glick Schiller, N., Basch, L. and Blanc-Szanton, C. (1992) 'Towards a definition of transnationalism', *Annals of the New York Academy of Sciences*, 645(1): DOI: 10.1111/j.1749-6632.1992.tb33482.x

Glick Schiller, N., Caglar, A. and Guldbrandsen, T.C. (2006) 'Beyond the ethnic lens: Locality, globality, and born–again incorporation', *American Ethnologist*, 33(4): 612–33.

Glick Schiller, N. and Salazar, N.B. (2013) 'Regimes of mobility across the globe', *Journal of Ethnic and Migration Studies*, 39(2): 183–200.

Gold, S.J. and Nawyn, S.J. (eds) (2013) *Routledge International Handbook of Migration Studies*, New York: Routledge.

Goldring, L. (1998/2017) 'The power of status in transnational social fields', in M.P. Smith and L.E. Guarnizo (eds), *Transnationalism from Below*, New York: Routledge, pp 165–95.

Greene, A.M. and Kirton, G. (2015) *The Dynamics of Managing Diversity: A Critical Approach*, Routledge.

Guarnizo, L.E. (1997) 'The emergence of a transnational social formation and the mirage of return migration among Dominican transmigrants', *Identities Global Studies in Culture and Power*, 4(2): 281–322.

Guo, G. and Al Ariss, A. (2015) 'Human resource management of international migrants: current theories and future research', *The International Journal of Human Resource Management*, 26(10): 1287–97.

Gupta, A.K. and Govindarajan, V. (2002) 'Cultivating a global mindset', *The Academy of Management Executive*, 16(1): 116–26.

Gusterson, H. (2017) 'From Brexit to Trump: Anthropology and the rise of nationalist populism', *American Ethnologist*, 44(2): 209–14.

Gutiérrez, K.D., Baquedano-López, P. and Tejeda, C. (1999) 'Rethinking diversity: Hybridity and hybrid language practices in the third space', *Mind, Culture, and Activity*, 6(4): 286–303.

Guttormsen, D.S.A. and Lauring, J. (2018) 'Fringe voices in cross-cultural management research: Silenced and neglected?', *International Studies of Management and Organization*, 48(3): 239–46, DOI: 10.1080/00208825.2018.1480465

Hahamovitch, C. (2003) 'Creating perfect immigrants: Guestworkers of the world in historical perspective 1', *Labor History*, 44(1): 69–94.

Hajro, A. (2017) 'Integrating highly-qualified migrants: Allowing a personal narrative to set future research directions', *European Journal of Cross-cultural Competence and Management*, 4(3): 192–200.

Hajro, A., Gibson, C.B. and Pudelko, M. (2017) 'Knowledge exchange processes in multicultural teams: Linking organizational diversity climates to teams' effectiveness', *Academy of Management Journal*, 60(1): 345–72.

Hajro, A., Zilinskaite, M. and Stahl, G. (2017) 'Acculturation of highly-qualified migrants: Individual coping strategies and climate for inclusion', *Academy of Management Proceedings* (Vol. 2017, No. 1, p. 13666), Briarcliff Manor, NY: Academy of Management.

Hall, D. (2013) 'Primitive accumulation, accumulation by dispossession and the global land grab', *Third World Quarterly*, 34(9): 1582–604.

Hall, S. (2014) 'Cultural identity and diaspora', in N. Mirzoeff (ed), *Diaspora and Visual Culture*, New York: Routledge, pp 35–47.

Hall, S. (1994/2017) *Race, Ethnicity, Nation: The Fateful/Fatal Triangle*, WEB Du Bois Lecture, Hutchins Center for African and African American Research, Cambridge, MA: Harvard University.

Halverson, C.B. and Tirmizi, S.A. (eds) (2008) *Effective Multicultural Teams: Theory and Practice* (Vol. 3), Dordrecht: Springer Science and Business Media.

Hannerz, U. (2004) 'Cosmopolitanism', in D. Nugent and J. Vincent (eds), *A Companion to the Anthropology of Politics*, Oxford: Blackwell, pp 69–85.

Harrison, D.A., Shaffer, M.A. and Bhaskar-Shrinivas, P. (2004) 'Going places: Roads more and less traveled in research on expatriate experiences', in M.R. Buckley, J.R.B. Halbesleben, A.R. Wheeler (eds) *Research in Personnel and Human Resources Management*, ebook series, Emerald Group Publishing Limited, pp 199–247.

Hartmann, E., Feisel, E. and Schober, H. (2010) 'Talent management of western MNCs in China: Balancing global integration and local responsiveness', *Journal of World Business*, 45(2): 169–78.

Harvey, D. (2003) *The New Imperialism*, Oxford: Oxford University Press.

Harvey, D. (2006) *Spaces of Global Capitalism*, New York: Verso.

Held, D., McGrew, A., Goldblatt, D. and Perraton, J. (2000) 'Global transformations: Politics, economics and culture', in C. Pierson and S. Tormey (eds), *Politics at the Edge*, London: Palgrave Macmillan, pp 14–28.

Herring, C. (2009) 'Does diversity pay? Race, gender, and the business case for diversity', *American Sociological Review*, 74(2): 208–24.

Hofstede, G. (1980) 'Motivation, leadership, and organization: do American theories apply abroad?', *Organizational Dynamics*, 9(1): 42–63.

Hofstede, G. (1983) 'The cultural relativity of organizational practices and theories', *Journal of International Business Studies*, 14(2): 75–89.

Hofstede, G. (1984a) *Culture's Consequences: International Differences in Work-related Values* (Vol. 5), Thousand Oaks, CA: Sage Publications.

Hofstede, G. (1984b) 'Cultural dimensions in management and planning', *Asia Pacific Journal of Management*, 1(2): 81–99.

Hofstede, G. (1993) 'Cultural constraints in management theories', *The Academy of Management Executive*, 7(1): 81–94.

Hofstede, G. (2003) *Culture's Consequences: Comparing Values, Behaviors, Institutions and Organizations across Nations*, Thousand Oaks, CA: Sage Publications.

Hollimon, S.E. (2006) 'The archaeology of nonbinary genders in Native North American societies', in S.M. Nelson (ed), *Handbook of Gender in Archaeology*, Lanham, MD: Alta Mira Press, pp 435–50.

Holvino, E. (2010) 'Intersections: The simultaneity of race, gender and class in organization studies', *Gender, Work & Organization*, 17(3): 248–77.

Holvino, E. (2014) 'Developing multicultural organizations', in B.B. Jones and M. Brazzel (eds), *The NTL Handbook of Organization Development and Change*, San Francisco, CA: Wiley, pp 517–34.

Horwitz, S.K. and Horwitz, I.B. (2007) 'The effects of team diversity on team outcomes: A meta-analytic review of team demography', *Journal of Management*, 33(6): 987–1015.

Islam, S. (2013) 'Toward decolonizing methodologies for immigration research', in P. Kretsedemas, J. Capetillo-Ponce, and G. Jacobs (eds), *Migrant Marginality: A Transnational Perspective*, New York: Routledge, pp 309–23.

Isotalo, R. (2009) 'Politicizing the transnational: On implications for migrants, refugees, and scholarship', *Social Analysis*, 53(3): 60–84.

Jack, G.A., Calás, M.B., Nkomo, S.M. and Peltonen, T. (2008) 'Critique and international management: an uneasy relationship?', *Academy of Management Review*, 33(4): 870–84.

Jack, G., Zhu, Y., Barney, J., Brannen, M.Y., Prichard, C., Singh, K. and Whetten, D. (2013) 'Refining, reinforcing and reimagining universal and indigenous theory development in international management', *Journal of Management Inquiry*, 22(2): 148–64.

Jackson, T. (2004) *Management and Change in Africa: A Cross-cultural Perspective*, New York: Routledge.

Jacques, R. (2015) 'The short life and premature death of critical "diversity" research', in A. Prasad, P. Prasad, A.J. Mills, and J. Helms Mills (eds), *The Routledge Companion to Critical Management Studies*, New York: Routledge, pp 140–58.

Janssens, M. and Zanoni, P. (2014) 'Alternative diversity management: Organizational practices fostering ethnic equality at work', *Scandinavian Journal of Management*, 30(3): 317–31.

Johnson, E. (2013) *Resistance and Empowerment in Black Women's Hair Styling*, New York: Routledge.

Johnson, T.A. and Bankhead, T. (2014) 'Hair it is: Examining the experiences of Black women with natural hair', *Open Journal of Social Sciences*, 2: 86–100.

Johnson, E.C., Kristof-Brown, A.L. and Klein, M.R. (2003) 'Expatriate social ties: Personality antecedents and consequences for adjustment', *International Journal of Selection and Assessment*, 11(4): 277–88.

Johnson, J.P., Lenartowicz, T. and Apud, S. (2006) 'Cross-cultural competence in international business: Toward a definition and a model', *Journal of International Business Studies*, 37(4): 525–43.

Jonsen, K. (2018) 'Beyond nation-state thinking and other stubborn facts in cross-cultural research', *International Studies of Management and Organization*, 48(3): 277–93.

Jonsen, K., Maznevski, M.L. and Schneider, S.C. (2011) 'Special review article: Diversity and its not so diverse literature: An international perspective', *International Journal of Cross Cultural Management*, 11(1): 35–62.

Joppke, C. and Morawska, E. (2014) 'Integrating immigrants in liberal nation-states: Policies and practices', in C. Joppke and E. Morawska (eds), *Toward Assimilation and Citizenship: Immigrants in Liberal Nation-states*, London: Palgrave Macmillan, pp 1–36.

Joshi, A. and Roh, H. (2009) 'The role of context in work team diversity research: A meta-analytic review', *Academy of Management Journal*, 52(3): 599–627.

Kalev, A., Dobbin, F. and Kelly, E. (2006) 'Best practices or best guesses? Diversity management and the remediation of inequality', *American Sociological Review*, 71(4): 589–617.

Kalir, B. (2013) 'Moving subjects, stagnant paradigms: Can the "mobilities paradigm" transcend methodological nationalism?', *Journal of Ethnic and Migration Studies*, 39(2): 311–27.

Kalonaityte, V. (2010) 'The case of vanishing borders: Theorizing diversity management as internal border control', *Organization*, 17(1): 31–52.

Kalra, V., Kaur, R. and Hutnyk, J. (2005) *Diaspora and Hybridity*, Thousand Oaks, CA: Sage.

Kamrava, M. and Babar, Z. (eds) (2012) *Migrant Labor in the Persian Gulf*, Columbia, NY: Hurst.

Karraker, M.W. (ed) (2013) *The Other People: Interdisciplinary Perspectives on Migration*, Cham, Switzerland: Springer.

Katz-Gerro, T. (2017) 'Cross-national differences in the consumption of non-national culture in Europe', *Cultural Sociology*, 11(4): 438–67.

Kendall-Taylor, A., Frantz, E. and Wright, J. (2017) 'The global rise of personalized politics: It's not just dictators anymore', *The Washington Quarterly*, 40(1): 7–19.

Khagram, S. and Levitt, P. (2007) *The Transnational Studies Reader: Intersections and Innovations*, New York: Routledge.

Kilduff, M., Angelmar, R. and Mehra, A. (2000) 'Top management-team diversity and firm performance: Examining the role of cognitions', *Organization Science*, 11(1): 21–34.

Kingfisher, C. and Maskovsky, J. (2008) 'Introduction: The limits of neoliberalism', *Critique of Anthropology*, 28(2): 115–26.

Koehn, P.H. and Rosenau, J.N. (2002) 'Transnational competence in an emergent epoch', *International Studies Perspectives*, 3(2): 105–27.

Kong, L. (2014) 'Transnational mobilities and the making of creative cities', *Theory, Culture and Society*, 31(7–8): 273–89.

Konrad, A. M., Prasad, P. and Pringle, J. (eds) (2005) *Handbook of Workplace Diversity*, Sage.

Koopmans, R. (ed) (2005) *Contested Citizenship: Immigration and Cultural Diversity in Europe* (Vol. 25), Minneapolis, MN: University of Minnesota Press.

Kretsedemas, P., Capetillo-Ponce, J. and Jacobs, G. (eds) (2013) *Migrant Marginality: A Transnational Perspective*, New York: Routledge.

Kuhn, T. (1962) *The Structure of Scientific Revolutions,* Chicago, IL: University of Chicago.

Kumar, P. (ed) (2017) *Exploring Dynamic Mentoring Models in India*, Cham, Switzerland: Palgrave Macmillan.

Kuo, L. (2018) 'Hong Kong bans pro-independence party as China tightens its grip', *Guardian*, 24 September, www.theguardian.com/world/2018/sep/24/hong-kong-bans-pro-independence-party-as-china-tightens-grip

Latour, B. (2012) *We Have Never Been Modern*, Cambridge, MA: Harvard University Press.

Lauring, J. (2009) 'Managing cultural diversity and the process of knowledge sharing: A case from Denmark', *Scandinavian Journal of Management*, 25(4): 385–94.

Lauring, J. and Selmer, J. (2012) 'International language management and diversity climate in multicultural organizations', *International Business Review*, 21(2): 156–66.

Leonard, P. (2010) 'Organizing whiteness: Gender, nationality and subjectivity in postcolonial Hong Kong', *Gender, Work and Organization*, 17(3): 340–58.

Leone, L., Van der Zee, K.I., van Oudenhoven, J.P., Perugini, M. and Ercolani, A.P. (2005) 'The cross-cultural generalizability and validity of the Multicultural Personality Questionnaire', *Personality and Individual Differences*, 38(6): 1449–62.

Levitt, P. (2012) 'What's wrong with migration scholarship? A critique and a way forward', *Identities: Global Studies in Culture and Power*, 19(4): 493–500.

Levitt, P. and Glick Schiller, N. (2004) 'Conceptualizing simultaneity: A transnational social field perspective on society', *International Migration Review*, 38(3): 1002–39.

Levitt, P. and Jaworsky, B.N. (2007) 'Transnational migration studies: Past developments and future trends', *Annual Review of Sociology*, 33: 129–56.

Levitt, P., DeWind, J. and Vertovec, S. (2003) 'International perspectives on transnational migration: An introduction', *International Migration Review*, 37(3): 565–75.

Levy, D.L. (2008) 'Political contestation in global production networks', *Academy of Management Review*, 33(4): 943–63.

Levy, O., Beechler, S., Taylor, S. and Boyacigiller, N.A. (2007) 'What we talk about when we talk about "global mindset": Managerial cognition in multinational corporations', *Journal of International Business Studies*, 38(2): 231–58.

Lewis, H., Dwyer, P., Hodkinson, S. and Waite, L. (2015) 'Hyper-precarious lives: Migrants, work and forced labour in the Global North', *Progress in Human Geography*, 39(5): 580–600.

Ley, D. (2004) 'Transnational spaces and everyday lives', *Transactions of the Institute of British Geographers*, 29(2): 151–64.

Lind, E.A. and Tyler, T.R. (1988) *The Social Psychology of Procedural Justice*, Cham: Springer Science and Business Media.

Liu, H. (2016a) 'Beneath the white gaze: Strategic self-Orientalism among Chinese Australians', *Human Relations*, 70(7): 781–804, DOI: 10.1177/0018726716676323

Liu, H. (2016b) 'Undoing Whiteness: The Dao of Anti-racist Diversity Practice', *Gender, Work and Organization*, 24(5): 457–71, DOI: 10.1111/gwao.12142

Lorbiecki, A. and Jack, G. (2000) 'Critical turns in the evolution of diversity management', *British Journal of Management*, 11: S17–S31.

Lorde, A. (1984/2012) *Sister Outsider: Essays and Speeches*, Crossing Press.

Lutz, H. (2016) 'Introduction: Migrant domestic workers in Europe', in H. Lutz (ed), *Migration and Domestic Work*, New York: Routledge, pp 13–22.

Lynch, F.R. (2017) *The Diversity Machine: The Drive to Change the White Male Workplace*, New York: Routledge.

Mahadevan, J. and Kilian-Yasin, K. (2017) 'Dominant discourse, orientalism and the need for reflexive HRM: Skilled Muslim migrants in the German context', *The International Journal of Human Resource Management*, 28(8): 1140–62.

Mahadevan, J. and Mayer, C.H. (eds) (2017) *Muslim Minorities, Workplace Diversity and Reflexive HRM*, New York, NY: Taylor and Francis.

Mai, N. (2013) 'Embodied cosmopolitanisms: The subjective mobility of migrants working in the global sex industry', *Gender, Place and Culture*, 20(1): 107–24.

Mannix, E., and Neale, M.A. (2005) 'What differences make a difference? The promise and reality of diverse teams in organizations', *Psychological Science in the Public Interest*, 6(2): 31–55.

Marcus, G.E. (1995) 'Ethnography in/of the world system: The emergence of multi-sited ethnography', *Annual Review of Anthropology*, 24(1): 95–117.

McCall, L. (2005) 'The complexity of intersectionality', *Signs*, 30(3): 1771–800.

McCorkel, J.A. and Myers, K. (2003) 'What difference does difference make? Position and privilege in the field', *Qualitative Sociology*, 26(2): 199–231.

McDowell, L. (2008) 'Thinking through work: Complex inequalities, constructions of difference and trans-national migrants', *Progress in Human Geography*, 32(4): 491–507.

McFarlin, D.B. and Sweeney, P.D. (1992) 'Distributive and procedural justice as predictors of satisfaction with personal and organizational outcomes', *Academy of Management Journal*, 35(3): 626–37.

McKenna, S., Ravishankar, M.N. and Weir, D. (2015) 'Critical perspectives on the globally mobile professional and managerial class', *Critical Perspectives on International Business*, 11(2): 118–21.

McLaughlin, J., Wells, D., Mendiburo, A., Lyn, A. and Vasilevska, B. (2017) '"Temporary workers", temporary fathers: Transnational family impacts of Canada's seasonal agricultural worker program', *Relations Industrielles/Industrial Relations*, 72(4): 682–709.

McLeod, P.L., Lobel, S.A. and Cox Jr, T.H. (1996) 'Ethnic diversity and creativity in small groups', *Small Group Research*, 27(2): 248–64.

McNulty, Y. and Brewster, C. (2017) 'Theorizing the meaning(s) of "expatriate": Establishing boundary conditions for business expatriates', *The International Journal of Human Resource Management*, 28(1): 27–61.

Meissner, F. (2015) 'Migration in migration-related diversity? The nexus between superdiversity and migration studies', *Ethnic and Racial Studies*, 38(4): 556–67.

Mendieta, E. (2009) 'From imperial to dialogical cosmopolitanism', *Ethics and Global Politics*, 2(3): 241–58.

Michaels, W.B. (2016) *The Trouble with Diversity: How we Learned to Love Identity and Ignore Inequality*, New York: Macmillan.

Migration Policy Institute (2017) www.migrationpolicy.org/programs/data-hub/international-migration-statistics, accessed October 18, 2018.

Milkman, R. (2013) 'Immigrant workers, precarious work, and the US labor movement', in R. Munck, C.U. Schierup and R.D. Wise (eds), *Migration, Work and Citizenship in the New Global Order*, New York: Routledge, pp 121–32.

Milliken, F.J. and Martins, L.L. (1996) 'Searching for common threads: Understanding the multiple effects of diversity in organizational groups', *Academy of Management Review*, 21(2): 402–33.

Mishra, S. and Shirazi, F. (2010) 'Hybrid identities: American Muslim women speak', *Gender, Place and Culture*, 17(2): 191–209.

Mor Barak, M.E. (2016) *Managing Diversity: Toward a Globally Inclusive Workplace*, Thousand Oaks, CA: Sage Publications.

Moroşanu, L. (2018) 'Researching migrants' diverse social relationships: From ethnic to cosmopolitan sociability?', *The Sociological Review*, 66(1): 155–73.

Ndobo, A., Faure, A., Boisselier, J. and Giannaki, S. (2017) 'The ethno-racial segmentation jobs: The impacts of the occupational stereotypes on hiring decisions', *The Journal of Social Psychology*, 158(6): 663–79.

Ng, E.S. and Burke, R.J. (2005) 'Person–organization fit and the war for talent: Does diversity management make a difference?', *The International Journal of Human Resource Management*, 16(7): 1195–210.

Nguyen, A.M.D. and Benet-Martínez, V. (2010) 'Multicultural identity: What it is and why it matters', in R.J. Crisp (ed), *The Psychology of Social and Cultural Diversity*, Malden, MA: Wiley-Blackwell, pp 87–114.

Nguyen, A.M.D. and Benet-Martínez, V. (2013) 'Biculturalism and adjustment: A meta-analysis', *Journal of Cross-Cultural Psychology*, 44(1): 122–59.

Nguyen, K.Y.T., Smallidge, D.L., Boyd, L.D. and Rainchuso, L. (2017) 'Vietnamese oral health beliefs and practices: Impact on the utilization of western preventive oral health care', *American Dental Hygienists' Association*, 91(1): 49–56.

Nishii, L.H. (2013) 'The benefits of climate for inclusion for gender-diverse groups', *Academy of Management Journal*, 56(6): 1754–74.

Nkomo, S.M. (1992) 'The emperor has no clothes: Rewriting "race in organizations"', *Academy of Management Review*, 17(3): 487–513.

Nkomo, S.M. (2011) 'A postcolonial and anti-colonial reading of "African" leadership and management in organization studies: Tensions, contradictions and possibilities', *Organization*, 18(3): 365–86.

Nkomo, S. and Hoobler, J.M. (2014) 'A historical perspective on diversity ideologies in the United States: Reflections on human resource management research and practice', *Human Resource Management Review*, 24(3): 245–57.

Noon, M. (2018) 'Pointless diversity training: Unconscious bias, new racism and agency', *Work, Employment and Society*, 32(1): 198–209.

North, D.C. (1991) 'Institutions', *Journal of Economic Perspectives*, 5(1): 97–112.

Nowicka, M. and Kaweh, R. (2009) 'Looking at the practice of UN professionals: Strategies for managing differences and the emergence of a cosmopolitan identity', in M. Rovisco and M. Nowicka (eds), *Cosmopolitanism in Practice*, New York: Routledge, pp 51–71.

Nyambegera, S.M. (2002) 'Ethnicity and human resource management practice in sub-Saharan Africa: The relevance of the managing diversity discourse', *International Journal of Human Resource Management*, 13(7): 1077–90.

Okazaki, S., David, E.J.R. and Abelmann, N. (2008) 'Colonialism and psychology of culture', *Social and Personality Psychology Compass*, 2(1): 90–106.

Ong, A. (1999) *Flexible Citizenship: The Cultural Logics of Transnationality*, Berkeley, CA: University of California Press.

Ong, A. and Collier, S.J. (eds) (2008) *Global Assemblages: Technology, Politics, and Ethics as Anthropological Problems*, Malden, MA: Blackwell.

Özbilgin, M.F., Beauregard, T.A., Tatli, A. and Bell, M.P. (2011) 'Work–life, diversity and intersectionality: A critical review and research agenda', *International Journal of Management Reviews*, 13(2): 177–18.

Özbilgin, M., and Chanlat, J.F. (eds) (2017) *Management and Diversity: Perspectives from Different National Contexts*, Bingley: Emerald Group Publishing.

Özbilgin, M. and Tatli, A. (2008) *Global Diversity Management: An Evidence Based Approach*, New York: Palgrave Macmillan.

Özkazanç-Pan, B. (2008) 'International management research meets "the rest of the world"', *Academy of Management Review*, 33(4): 964–74.

Özkazanç-Pan, B. (2015) 'Postcolonial perspectives on cross-cultural management knowledge', in N. Holden, S. Michailova and S. Tietze, (eds), *Routledge Companion to Cross-cultural Management*, New York: Routledge, pp 371–79.

Özkazanç-Pan, B. (2018) 'CSR as gendered neocoloniality in the Global South', *Journal of Business Ethics*, https://doi.org/10.1007/s10551-018-3798-1

Özkazanç-Pan, B. (2019) '"Superdiversity": A new paradigm for inclusion in a transnational world', *Equality, Diversity and Inclusion: An International Journal*, 38(4): 477–90.

Özkazanç-Pan, B. and Calás, M.B. (2015) 'From here to there and back again: Transnational perspectives on diversity in organizations', in R. Bendl, I. Bleijenbergh, E. Henttonen and A.J. Mills (eds), *The Oxford Handbook of Diversity in Organizations*, Oxford: Oxford University Press, pp 575–602.

Page, S.E. (2008) *The Difference: How the Power of Diversity Creates Better Groups, Firms, Schools, and Societies*, Princeton, NJ: Princeton University Press.

Papastergiadis, N. (2018) *The Turbulence of Migration: Globalization, Deterritorialization and Hybridity*, Malden, MA: Blackwell.

Park, S.S. and Waldinger, R.D. (2016) 'Bridging the territorial divide: immigrants' cross-border communication and the spatial dynamics of their kin networks', *Journal of Ethnic and Migration Studies*, 43(1): 18–40.

Parker, M. (2018) *Shut Down the Business School*, Chicago, IL: University of Chicago Press Economics Books.

Parrenas, R.S. (2001) 'Transgressing the nation-state: The partial citizenship and "imagined (global) community" of migrant Filipina domestic workers', *Signs: Journal of Women in Culture and Society*, 26(4): 1129–54.

Pattie, M. and Parks, L. (2011) 'Adjustment, turnover, and performance: the deployment of minority expatriates', *The International Journal of Human Resource Management*, 22(10): 2262–80.

Peltonen, T. (2006) 'Critical theoretical perspectives on international human resource management', in G.K. Stahl, I. Björkman, and S. Morris (eds), *Handbook of Research in International Human Resource Management*, Northampton, MA: Edward Elgar, pp 532–48.

Peterson, B.D., Pandya, S.S. and Leblang, D. (2014) 'Doctors with borders: occupational licensing as an implicit barrier to high skill migration', *Public Choice*, 160(1–2): 45–63.

Peterson, M.F., Søndergaard, M. and Kara, A. (2017) 'Traversing cultural boundaries in IB: The complex relationships between explicit country and implicit cultural group boundaries at multiple levels', *Journal of International Business Studies*, 49(8): 1081–99, https://doi.org/10.1057/s41267-017-0082-z

Pieterse, A.N., Van Knippenberg, D. and Van Dierendonck, D. (2013) 'Cultural diversity and team performance: The role of team member goal orientation', *Academy of Management Journal*, 56(3): 782–804.

Pinder, C.C. (2014) *Work Motivation in Organizational Behaviour*, New York, NY: Psychology Press.

Pittinsky, T.L. and Shih, M.J. (2004) 'Knowledge nomads: Organizational commitment and worker mobility in positive perspective', *American Behavioral Scientist*, 47(6): 791–807.

Portes, A. (1997) 'Immigration theory for a new century: Some problems and opportunities', *International Migration Review*, 31(4): 799–825.

Portes, A., Guarnizo, L.E. and Landolt, P. (1999) 'The study of transnationalism: pitfalls and promise of an emergent research field', *Ethnic and Racial Studies*, 22(2): 217–37.

Portes, A. and Haller, W. (2010) 'The informal economy', in N.J. Smelser and R. Swedberg (eds), *The Handbook of Economic Sociology*, Princeton, NJ: Princeton University Press, pp 403–28.

Prasad, P., Mills, A.J., Elmes, M.B. and Prasad, A. (1997). *Managing the Organizational Melting Pot: Dilemmas of Workplace Diversity*, Thousand Oaks, CA: Sage.

Prasad, A., Prasad, P. and Mir, R. (2011). 'One mirror in another': Managing diversity and the discourse of fashion. *Human Relations*, 64(5), 703–24.

Pries, L. (2001) 'The approach of transnational social spaces: responding to new configurations of the social and the spatial', in L. Pries (ed), *New Transnational Social Spaces: International Migration and Transnational Companies in the Early Twenty-first Century*, New York: Routledge, pp 3–33.

Pries, L. (ed) (2008) *Rethinking Transnationalism: The Meso-link of Organisations*, New York: Routledge.

Primecz, H., Mahadevan, J. and Romani, L. (2016) 'Why is cross-cultural management scholarship blind to power relations? Investigating ethnicity, language, gender and religion in power-laden contexts', *International Journal of Cross Cultural Management*, 16(2):127–36.

Proudfoot, D. and Lind, E.A. (2015) 'Fairness heuristic theory, the uncertainty management model, and fairness at work', in R.S. Cropanzano and M.L. Ambrose (eds), *The Oxford Handbook of Justice in the Workplace*, Oxford: Oxford University Press, pp 371–86.

Prudham, S. (2007) 'The fictions of autonomous invention: Accumulation by dispossession, commodification and life patents in Canada', *Antipode*, 39(3): 406–29.

Ragins, B.R. (1997) 'Diversified mentoring relationships in organizations: A power perspective', *Academy of Management Review*, 22(2): 482–521.

Ralston, D.A., Holt, D.H., Terpstra, R.H. and Kai-Cheng, Y. (1997) 'The impact of national culture and economic ideology on managerial work values: A study of the United States, Russia, Japan, and China', *Journal of International Business Studies*, 28(1): 177–207.

Ratha, D. and Shaw, W. (2007) *South-South Migration and Remittances*, Washington, DC: The World Bank.

Ressia, S., Strachan, G. and Bailey, J. (2017) 'Operationalizing intersectionality: An approach to uncovering the complexity of the migrant job search in Australia', *Gender, Work and Organization*, 24(4): 376–97.

Risberg, A. and Soderberg, A.M. (2008) 'Translating a management concept: diversity management in Denmark', *Gender in Management: An International Journal*, 23(6): 426–41.

Roberson, Q., Holmes IV, O. and Perry, J.L. (2017) 'Transforming research on diversity and firm performance: A dynamic capabilities perspective', *Academy of Management Annals,* 11(1): 189–216.

Robinson, G. and Dechant, K. (1997) 'Building a business case for diversity', *The Academy of Management Executive*, 11(3): 21–31.

Rodriguez, J.K., Holvino, E., Fletcher, J.K. and Nkomo, S.M. (2016) 'The theory and praxis of intersectionality in work and organisations: Where do we go from here?', *Gender, Work and Organization*, 23(3): 201–22.

Rose, C. (2007) 'Does female board representation influence firm performance? The Danish evidence', *Corporate Governance: An International Review*, 15(2): 404–13.

Rose, N. (2009) *The Politics of Life Itself: Biomedicine, Power, and Subjectivity in the Twenty-first Century*, Princeton, NJ: Princeton University Press.

Rowley, C. and Harry, W. (2011) *Managing People Globally: An Asian Perspective*, Oxford: Chandos Publishing.

Rupp, D.E. Shapiro, D.L., Folger, R., Skarlicki, D.P. and Shao, R. (2017) 'A critical analysis of the conceptualization and measurement of organizational justice: Is it time for reassessment?', *Academy of Management Annals*, 11(2): 919–59.

Saldívar-Hull, S. (2000) *Feminism on the Border: Chicana Gender Politics and Literature*, Berkeley, CA: University of California Press.

Sarpel, U., Huang, X., Austin, C. and Gany, F. (2018) 'Barriers to care in Chinese immigrants with hepatocellular carcinoma: A focus group study in New York City', *Journal of Community Health*, 43(6): 1–11.

Sassen, S. (2011) *Cities in a World Economy*, Thousand Oaks, CA: Sage Publications.

Saxenian, A. (2005) 'From brain drain to brain circulation: Transnational communities and regional upgrading in India and China', *Studies in Comparative International Development (SCID)*, 40(2): 35–61.

Saxenian, A., Motoyama, Y. and Quan, X. (2002) *Local and Global Networks of Immigrant Professionals in Silicon Valley*, San Francisco, CA: Public Policy Institute of CA.

Scheele, R., Kearney, N.M., Kurniawan, J.H. and Schweizer, V.J. (2018) 'What scenarios are you missing? Poststructuralism for deconstructing and reconstructing organizational futures', in H. Kramer and M. Wenzel (eds), *How Organizations Manage the Future*, Cham: Palgrave Macmillan, pp 153–72.

Scholtz, C. (2013) *Negotiating Claims: The Emergence of Indigenous Land Claim Negotiation Policies in Australia, Canada, New Zealand, and the United States*, New York: Routledge.

Schuler, R.S., Budhwar, P.S. and Florkowski, G.W. (2002) 'International human resource management: review and critique', *International Journal of Management Reviews*, 4(1): 41–70.

Schultz, M., Maguire, S., Langley, A. and Tsoukas, H. (eds) (2012) *Constructing Identity in and around Organizations*, Oxford: Oxford University Press.

Schwartz, S.H. (1999) 'A theory of cultural values and some implications for work', *Applied Psychology*, 48(1): 23–47.

Selmer, J. and Lauring, J. (2015) 'Host country language ability and expatriate adjustment: The moderating effect of language difficulty', *The International Journal of Human Resource Management*, 26(3): 401–20.

Shaffer, M., Kraimer, M., Chen, Y.P. and Bolino, M.C. (2012) 'Choices, challenges, and career consequences of global work experiences: A review and future agenda', *Journal of Management*, 38(4): 1282–327.

Shen, J., Chanda, A., D'Netto, B., and Monga, M. (2009) 'Managing diversity through human resource management: An international perspective and conceptual framework', *The International Journal of Human Resource Management*, 20(2): 235–51.

Shenkar, O. (2001) 'Cultural distance revisited: Towards a more rigorous conceptualization and measurement of cultural differences', *Journal of International Business Studies*, 32(3): 519–35.

Shih, J. (2006) 'Circumventing discrimination: Gender and ethnic strategies in Silicon Valley', *Gender and Society*, 20(2): 177–206.

Shore, C. (2013) *Building Europe: The Cultural Politics of European Integration*, New York: Routledge.

Sklair, L. (2001) *The Transnational Capitalist Class*, Oxford: Blackwell.

Skovgaard-Smith, I. and Poulfelt, F. (2017) 'Imagining "non-nationality": Cosmopolitanism as a source of identity and belonging', *Human Relations*, 71(2): 129–54, DOI: 0018726717714042.

Skrbis, Z., Kendall, G. and Woodward, I. (2004) 'Locating cosmopolitanism: Between humanist ideal and grounded social category', *Theory, Culture and Society*, 21(6): 115–36.

Smith, J., Chatfield, C. and Pagnucco, R. (eds) (1997) *Transnational Social Movements and Global Politics: Solidarity Beyond the State*, Syracuse, NY: Syracuse University Press.

Smith, P.B., Dugan, S. and Trompenaars, F. (1996) 'National culture and the values of organizational employees: A dimensional analysis across 43 nations', *Journal of Cross-cultural Psychology*, 27(2): 231–64.

Snel, E., Engbersen, G. and Leerkes, A. (2006) 'Transnational involvement and social integration', *Global Networks*, 6(3): 285–308.

Srikanth, K., Harvey, S. and Peterson, R. (2016) 'A dynamic perspective on diverse teams: Moving from the dual-process model to a dynamic coordination-based model of diverse team performance', *Academy of Management Annals*, 10(1): 453–93.

Stahl, G.K., Björkman, I. and Morris, S. (eds) (2012) *Handbook of Research in International Human Resource Management*, Northampton, MA: Edward Elgar Publishing.

Steyn, M. (2005) '"White Talk": White South Africans and the management of diasporic Whiteness', in A.J. Lopez (ed), *Postcolonial Whiteness: A Reader on Race and Empire*, Albany, NY: State University of New York Press, pp 119–36.

Story, J.S. and Barbuto Jr, J.E. (2011) 'Global mindset: A construct clarification and framework', *Journal of Leadership and Organizational Studies*, 18(3): 377–84.

Syed, J. and Özbilgin, M. (2009) 'A relational framework for international transfer of diversity management practices', *The International Journal of Human Resource Management*, 20(12): 2435–53.

Syed, J. and Özbilgin, M. (eds) (2015) *Managing Diversity and Inclusion: An International Perspective*, Thousand Oaks, CA: Sage.

Syed, J. and Pio, E. (2010) 'Veiled diversity? Workplace experiences of Muslim women in Australia', *Asia Pacific Journal of Management*, 27(1): 115–37.

Tadmor, C.T., Galinsky, A.D. and Maddux, W.W. (2012) 'Getting the most out of living abroad: Biculturalism and integrative complexity as key drivers of creative and professional success', *Journal of Personality and Social Psychology*, 103(3): 520–42.

Tams, S. and Arthur, M.B. (2007) 'Studying careers across cultures: Distinguishing international, cross-cultural, and globalization perspectives', *Career Development International*, 12(1): 86–98.

Taras, V., Kirkman, B.L. and Steel, P. (2010) 'Examining the impact of Culture's consequences: A three-decade, multilevel, meta-analytic review of Hofstede's cultural value dimensions', *Journal of Applied Psychology*, 95(3): 405–39.

Tatli, A., and Özbilgin, M.F. (2012) 'An emic approach to intersectional study of diversity at work: A Bourdieuan framing', *International Journal of Management Reviews*, 14(2): 180–200.

Taylor, C. (ed) (1994) *Multiculturalism*, Princeton, NJ: Princeton University Press.

Thomas, D.C., Brannen, M.Y. and Garcia, D. (2010) 'Bicultural individuals and intercultural effectiveness', *European Journal of Cross-Cultural Competence and Management*, 1(4): 315–33.

Thompson, N. (2016) *Anti-discriminatory Practice: Equality, Diversity and Social Justice*, Cham: Palgrave Macmillan.

Tomaskovic-Devey, D. (2014) 'The relational generation of workplace inequalities', *Social Currents*, 1(1): 51–73.

Tomlinson, F. and Schwabenland, C. (2010) 'Reconciling competing discourses of diversity? The UK non-profit sector between social justice and the business case', *Organization*, 17(1): 101–21.

Trefry, M.G. (2006) 'A double-edged sword: Organizational culture in multicultural organizations', *International Journal of Management*, 23(3): 563–75.

Tsui, A.S., Egan, T.D. and O'Reilly III, C.A. (1992) 'Being different: Relational demography and organizational attachment', *Administrative Science Quarterly*, 37(4): 549–79.

Tung, R.L. (2008a) 'The cross-cultural research imperative: The need to balance cross-national and intra-national diversity', *Journal of International Business Studies*, 39(1): 41–6.

Tung, R.L. (2008b) 'Brain circulation, diaspora, and international competitiveness', *European Management Journal*, 26(5): 298–304.

Tung, R.L. (2016) 'New perspectives on human resource management in a global context', *Journal of World Business*, 51(1): 142–52.

United Nations (2017) *International Migration Report*, www.un.org/en/development/desa/population/migration/publications/migrationreport/docs/MigrationReport2017_Highlights.pdf

USCIS (United States Citizenship and Immigration Services) (2018) 'Immigration and citizenship data', www.uscis.gov/tools/reports-studies/immigration-forms-data

Van den Brink, M., Benschop, Y. and Jansen, W. (2010) 'Transparency in academic recruitment: A problematic tool for gender equality?', *Organization Studies*, 31(11), 1459–83.

Van Knippenberg, D., De Dreu, C.K. and Homan, A.C. (2004) 'Work group diversity and group performance: An integrative model and research agenda', *Journal of Applied Psychology*, 89(6): 1008–22.

Van Laer, K. and Janssens, M. (2011) 'Ethnic minority professionals' experiences with subtle discrimination in the workplace', *Human Relations*, 64(9): 1203–27.

Van Laer, K. and Janssens, M. (2014) 'Between the devil and the deep blue sea: Exploring the hybrid identity narratives of ethnic minority professionals', *Scandinavian Journal of Management*, 30(2): 186–96.

Van Laer, K. and Janssens, M. (2017) 'Agency of ethnic minority employees: Struggles around identity, career and social change', *Organization*, 24(2): 198–217.

Vertovec, S. (2001) 'Transnational challenges to the 'new' multiculturalism', *ASA conference*, Vol. 30, www.transcomm.ox.ac.uk/working%20papers/WPTC-2K-06%20Vertovec.pdf

Vertovec, S. (2007) 'Super-diversity and its implications', *Ethnic and Racial Studies*, 30(6): 1024–54.

Vertovec, S. (2009) *Transnationalism*, New York: Routledge.

Vertovec, S. and Cohen, R. (eds) (2003) *Conceiving Cosmopolitanism: Theory, Context and Practice*, Oxford: Oxford University Press.

Vora, N. (2008) 'Producing diasporas and globalization: Indian middle-class migrants in Dubai', *Anthropological Quarterly*, 81(2): 377–406.

Waldinger, R. (2013) 'Immigrant transnationalism', *Current Sociology*, 61(5–6): 756–77.

Waldinger, R. and Fitzgerald, D. (2004) 'Transnationalism in question', *American Journal of Sociology*, 109(5): 1177–95.

Wang, L. (2007) 'Diaspora, identity and cultural citizenship: The Hakkas in "Multicultural Taiwan"', *Ethnic and Racial Studies*, 30(5): 875–95.

Waterbury, M.A. (2010) 'Bridging the divide: Towards a comparative framework for understanding kin state and migrant-sending state diaspora politics', in R. Bauböck, and T. Faist (eds), *Diaspora and Transnationalism: Concepts, Theories and Methods*, Amsterdam: Amsterdam University Press, pp 131–48.

Webb, J.W., Tihanyi, L., Ireland, R.D. and Sirmon, D.G. (2009) 'You say illegal, I say legitimate: Entrepreneurship in the informal economy', *Academy of Management Review*, 34(3): 492–510.

Wells, C.C., Gill, R. and McDonald, J. (2015) '"Us foreigners": Intersectionality in a scientific organization', *Equality, Diversity and Inclusion: An International Journal*, 34(6): 539–53.

Werbner, P. (2006) 'Vernacular cosmopolitanism', *Theory, Culture and Society*, 23(2–3): 496–98.

Williams, C.L., Kilanski, K. and Muller, C. (2014) 'Corporate diversity programs and gender inequality in the oil and gas industry', *Work and Occupations*, 41(4): 440–76.

Williams, K.Y. and O'Reilly III, C.A. (1998) 'A review of 40 years of research', *Research in Organizational Behavior*, 20: 77–140.

Willmott, H. (ed) (1992) *Critical Management Studies*, Thousand Oaks, CA: Sage.

Wimmer, A. and Glick Schiller, N. (2002) 'Methodological nationalism and beyond: Nation–state building, migration and the social sciences', *Global Networks*, 2(4): 301–34.

Wingfield, A.H. (2019) *Flatlining: Race, Work and Health Care in the New Economy*, Berkeley, CA: University of California Press.

Wingfield, A.H. and Alston, R.S. (2014) 'Maintaining hierarchies in predominantly White organizations: A theory of racial tasks', *American Behavioral Scientist*, 58(2), 274–87.

Witt, M.A. (2008) 'Crossvergence 10 years on: Impact and further potential', *Journal of International Business Studies*, 39(1): 47–52.

Wolf, E.R. (2010) *Europe and the People Without History*, Berkeley, CA: University of California Press.

Wooten, M.E. and Couloute, L. (2017) 'The production of racial inequality within and among organizations', *Sociology Compass*, 11(1): e12446.

Yagi, N. and Kleinberg, J. (2011) 'Boundary work: An interpretive ethnographic perspective on negotiating and leveraging cross-cultural identity', *Journal of International Business Studies*, 42(5): 629–53.

Young, R.J. (1995/2005) *Colonial Desire: Hybridity in Theory, Culture and Race*, New York: Routledge.

Yuval-Davis, N. (2006) 'Intersectionality and feminist politics', *European Journal of Women's Studies*, 13(3): 193–209.

Zambrana, R.E., Harvey Wingfield, A., Lapeyrouse, L.M., Dávila, B.A., Hoagland, T.L. and Valdez, R.B. (2017) 'Blatant, subtle, and insidious: URM faculty perceptions of discriminatory practices in predominantly white institutions', *Sociological Inquiry*, 87(2): 207–32.

Zanoni, P., Janssens, M., Benschop, Y. and Nkomo, S. (2010) 'Guest editorial: Unpacking diversity, grasping inequality: Rethinking difference through critical perspectives', *Organization*, 17(1): 9–29.

Zhang, Y. and Guo, Y. (2015) 'Becoming transnational: Exploring multiple identities of students in a Mandarin–English bilingual programme in Canada', *Globalisation, Societies and Education*, 13(2): 210–29.

Index